# YOUR TURN TO LEAD

A GUIDE FOR BIBLE DISCUSSION GROUPS
by Margaret Parker

SCRIPTURE UNION 5 WIGMORE STREET, LONDON W1H 0AD

ISBN 0 85421 385 6
Printed by A. McLay & Co. Ltd., Cardiff and London

# CONTENTS

# INTRODUCTION

## Mainly for the Inexperienced

The comments which follow are elementary and will be well-known to the experienced group Bible study leader. They are intended primarily for those who are considering leading a group for the first time, or who are inexperienced at it. However, even the more experienced leader may find it helpful to glance through these early pages in order to refresh his memory on the basics.

## Preparation 1 Personal

When taking on the responsibility of group Bible study leadership, whether it is as a permanent appointment or a once-and-for-all happening, a leader should not neglect personal preparation. He should have a deep love of the Bible and be increasingly familiar with it through his own regular reading. He needs a genuine concern that others should meet Jesus Christ and apply Biblical teaching to their lives. He must be prepared to pray for group members individually.

## 2 For the meeting

1   *Pray* about the meeting, asking that God will help you to prepare and lead it.

2   *Decide* what is the aim of the meeting. It may be introducing people to Jesus Christ, building up Christians, or teaching some particular truth. Keep the aim(s) in mind during your preparation and throughout the meeting.

3   If a passage has not been provided for you together with the mantle of leadership, *select* a suitable one. I have found that much valuable preparation time can be wasted in flicking over pages of the

4

Bible in the vague hope that a passage will present itself, and that it is quicker to select a section of the Bible (e.g. a gospel or an epistle), and determine to find a passage there. Alternatively, Appendix 2 of this book gives lists of passages suitable for group Bible study.

4   *Read* the selected passage several times in as many translations as are available in order to ensure familiarity with the content.

5   *Study* a commentary to acquire background information and to throw light on specific aspects of the passage. It is preferable to use one good commentary (see Bibliography) for basic study and to dip into others only for the clarification of specific points, as the reading of large numbers of lengthy commentaries can be confusing. Thoughtfully consider the possible practical applications of the teaching to be considered. Make notes as appropriate.

6   *Method.* When the meaning of the passage has been mastered, select a method of presentation to the group. The method should be appropriate both to your group and to the passage.

Section 1 of this book describes 16 possible methods, and Appendices 1 and 3 offer guidance on the selection of an appropriate one.

7   *Prepare the presentation* to the group, making notes on the procedure to be adopted at each stage, including information to be imparted, questions to be asked, division into smaller groups, the distribution of slips of paper, presentation of visual aids, etc. Work out a time schedule for each part of the meeting. Large sheets of notes behind which the leader hides are a little disconcerting for the group members, so make your notes as unobtrusive as possible. A small loose-leaf notebook is useful if leadership is undertaken regularly. The sheets can be taken out and slipped into the Bible for the duration of the meeting.

8   *Prepare visual aids*, slips of paper containing references, questions, etc.

9   *Work through* the meeting in your mind, checking that you know when and how to conduct each section.

10   *Check* that the room is available at the time required and that the meeting is advertised in an appropriate way. The most careful preparation is worthless if no one is aware that there is to be a meeting.

11   *Pray* again, for the meeting itself and for the group members by name, if known. Continue to re-read the passage and to pray until the day of the meeting.

Clearly, all this takes time, and it is vital to start the preparation early to allow for contingencies such as the loss of your favourite commentary, sudden illness, or other demands on your time. A hastily-prepared Bible study can be satisfactory, but a carefully prepared one is less likely to run into difficulties. If we have any respect for God and His word, we should be willing to allocate time for preparation.

# At the meeting

1 *(Beforehand) Arrive early to prepare the room*

(a)   Check for adequate light, heat and comfort. The heat and comfort should not be excessive as that can have a soporific effect; equally, cold and discomfort can be a distraction.

(b)   Arrange the seats. A circle is usually best as this avoids the impression that the leader is the fount of all knowledge.

(c)   Make sure that all visual aids are visible to the whole group.

(d)   Have available a set of Bibles, particularly if members are unlikely to bring their own. In any case, it can be helpful to have one version which is used by all members; in addition, have other translations available for reference.

2 *Welcome* members as they arrive.

If there are any newcomers, find out their names and if possible have a brief chat with them. You may be able to ascertain their degree of familiarity with Bible study groups. This will help you to know to what extent to draw them into the discussion. Even a veteran Bible study-er can be over-awed by a group where everyone else seems to know each other, so care should be taken to make him feel part of the group from the outset.

3 *Start* the meeting at the advertised time.

The friendly procedure of 'waiting until Peter arrives because he said he was coming' results in the meetings starting later and later week by week, because no one feels impelled to arrive on time. A prompt start with only a small percentage of the total group present can work wonders for the arrival time at the following meeting.

4 *Your attitude.*

(a)   As the meeting proceeds, try to keep the situation well under your own control. Acquire the technique of appearing well-organized without being officious. Teachers may find it harder than most to maintain a casual atmosphere!

(b)   An attitude of humility is appropriate. We do well to remind ourselves that we do not know all the answers, even though we may have spent many hours preparing a particular study. We need to come to the meeting willing to learn from others, and prepared to admit that our views may be wrong.

(c)   On the other hand, do not assume too much knowledge, particularly with a group of young people. If there is any doubt in your mind whether they will know, for instance, that Saul in Acts was the man later known as Paul, make sure you include that information. This may be done by a passing reference, or in a recapitulation of previous chapters, or in some other indirect way to avoid insulting the intelligence of those who do know.

(d)   Be absolutely unshockable. Whatever is said, listen, and deal with it as appropriate, but do not express shock. If the member is aiming to shock you and to cause trouble, it is best to disappoint him; if he is saying something he genuinely believes or is inclined to believe, it may be damaging to him for you to appear shocked. It is far better to let him have his say and then gently point him to a better way, or, even more helpfully, encourage other members to reason with him.

### 5 *Procedure*
The following procedure does not claim to be a blueprint for a successful meeting, but with appropriate modifications it can be taken as recommended general practice:

(a)   Prayer.

Unless the group would be inhibited or embarrassed by an opening prayer (and this would apply if the aim of the meeting was to start on general subjects and steer a somewhat unwilling group towards consideration of the Biblical viewpoint), it is helpful to start in this way. The prayer should be short and simple, asking God to teach members more about Himself and His way by means of the study of the passage, and asking for the leading and guidance of the Holy Spirit.

The prayer should not be a mini-sermon, either reminding the group of all their shortcomings, or pre-empting the study of its content. In many cases you can ask someone else to open (and later to close) in prayer, as this helps to involve more people in the leadership. Due warning should always be given to someone who is expected to participate in any way. It may be helpful to say 'I have already asked John to open in prayer and he will now do that.' There is no danger then of shy members staying away for fear of beingpounced on.

(b) Read the passage.

This may be done in a number of ways. One person may read the whole; several may take a paragraph each; or, in a dramatic passage, and where all the readers are using the same version, members may read the words of the participants with a narrator reading the rest. It is never advisable to 'read around' a verse at a time. Some members might be acutely embarrassed, for a variety of reasons, and most would have a quick glance at their own verse, thus losing the thread of the passage. If different versions are in use, confusion arises and concentration and understanding are lost. In order to get the most of one reading of the passage, it may be helpful for you to do any or all of the following:

(i)   Give a brief introduction, outlining the general subject-matter of the passage.

(ii)  Indicate the main points to be discussed subsequent to the reading.

(iii) Provide a question to be considered during the reading. The question needs to have an obvious answer, and could be something such as 'Notice how many things the passage indicates God has done for us'.

(c)   Unless this has already been done, give an introduction to the passage. This should provide relevant background information, but should not be long enough to encourage members to sit back passively, as it is difficult subsequently to jerk them out of their passivity into active vocal participation. The introduction should arouse interest and stimulate ideas. Avoid summarizing what the group is expected to learn.

(d)   It may be appropriate at this point to ask for questions, or to explain the meaning of any technical terms used in the passage.

(e)   Follow your planned method, mentally recapitulating every few minutes to ensure that you are not missing the main point, that too much time is not being spent on one section, and that the meeting is not being unnecessarily dominated by you or any other person.

(f)   Ensure that there is application of the teaching provided by the passage. For instance, when discussing Romans 12 verse 13, 'Contribute to the needs of the saints, practise hospitality', don't allow the group to avoid the real point at issue. It is easy to express verbal enthusiasm with general advice of this kind and promptly to forget it when the study closes. Make time for specific suggestions of practical ways for the group or individual to begin giving more thoughtfully and imaginatively and to use their homes creatively.

(g)   As the study is drawing to a close, provide opportunity for questions to be asked. If major problems emerge which cannot be dealt with in the time available, write them down and keep them — perhaps in a Question Box to be dealt with at some later date. Short queries can be dealt with at the time.

(h)   Summarize the findings — or ask someone else who is competent to do so — but do not repeat everything which has been said, and do not impute to the group thoughts which have merely been in your mind.

(i)   Close with prayer.

This practice will vary according to the group. It may be appropriate simply to say the grace together; or one member (who has been forewarned) can draw together the thoughts of the group in prayer form. A group of mature Christians may find it helpful to hold a period of silent and/or open prayer. Members should be encouraged to pray only briefly and the leader can help less experienced members by suggesting lines along which they might pray.

(j)   Close on time.

This will encourage people to come again and it is better for them to go home with a hunger for more rather than indigestion from a surfeit.

# Problems

You may be feeling by now that leading a group Bible study is a perfectly simple operation and that, if you adopt this procedure, nothing can go wrong. That is far from true! Many difficulties arise, some insoluble, some at least partially soluble with a little anticipation and forward planning.

## The silent group

It is daunting to face a group where mouths, and apparently minds, are firmly closed, and there may be a situation when even the most stalwart leader will feel he has been defeated by the silent majority!

Some methods are more suitable than others for this kind of group, and special care should be taken in selecting the method. (See Section 1). It can be helpful to adopt a method which demands group participation in the early stages to ensure that group members take part in some way. See Methods 5, 6, 7, 8 and 9. Equally, the Question and Answer method (Method 1) may be adopted, dividing the large group into two's and three's in the early stages of the study, so that members do not expect the leader to do all the talking. Some members will be more willing to express their thoughts to one other person than to the whole group, and they will gain confidence in this way. It may be helpful to have two leaders for a potentially silent group. If there are already two people participating, it is easier for others to join in.

If you have asked a question and sense that there will be no response, ask it again in another way, perhaps particularizing, so that someone can respond on that specific aspect of the subject.

If there is still no response, you can ask one of the 'old hands' (if any are present) what he thinks — but do not pounce on a newcomer, or he may be frightened off for good!

If the problem is merely that of breaking the ice, one or two members could be asked to read how their versions translate a particular verse. A 'planted' version comes into its own here, as you can say, 'I think the NEB put this rather well — can you tell us what it says, please, Ann?' This method may be adopted effectively with the quiet member of an articulate group, who may find that once his voice has been projected, he has the confidence to volunteer a thought of his own.

Try to appear relaxed (even if you feel very nervous) as the members are unlikely to relax sufficiently to discuss naturally if they sense that the leader is on edge.

## Over-talkative members

One member who will not stop talking can be as difficult as the silent ones! A sensitive person will respond to something like,

'Thank you, Andrew, but perhaps we can hear the views of someone who hasn't spoken yet.'

The less sensitive will need firmer treatment! Perhaps, 'Thank you, Alison, I think we are all fairly clear now about what you think so it would be a good idea to give someone else a chance to speak', will be effective. Or, 'Give the others a chance, Peter, they can't get a word in!'

If this approach does not restrain the talkative member, you may need to discuss it with him separately. You could point out to him that because he talks so much, the others are inclined just to leave it to him, or that they may feel inadequate because they cannot say as much. To appeal for his co-operation in involving more people in the discussions may be effective.

Failing all else, you could simply ask him to keep quiet for a while!

## The know-all

He may also be the over-talkative one, in which case you have a Big Problem! He will cause resentment and possible silence amongst the other members.

If his knowledge is helpful, encourage him to offer it from time to time, but try to prevent him from parading irrelevant facts purely to impress. A firm word such as 'That isn't quite on the subject, so we will leave it on one side for now, and concentrate on . . .' may silence him. The situation could be dealt with slightly humorously, with a comment such as, 'That's all very well for the erudite, John, but we simple folk need something rather different. Can anyone explain this verse in words that even I can understand?'

If he persists in airing his knowledge to the detriment of the group, try to talk to him about it after the study.

## Red herrings

There are two kinds. The red herrings which are thrown in purely as a diversion should be squashed immediately. If there is any suggestion that there may be some interest in the subject, note it down and deal with it on a future occasion.

The red herrings which cause real difficulty are the ones which arise from a deep personal problem which a member is anxious to share with the group. In this case, you need to decide promptly whether to

(a)   abandon the original programme and concentrate on the problem raised, or

(b)   give a few minutes to the problem with the intention of returning to the planned programme after a certain length of time, or

(c)   continue the meeting as planned but leave time at the end for consideration of the problem, or

(d)   insist on following the planned programme at all costs.

The decision depends on *the nature of the problem*, whether it is suitable for general discussion with that particular group, or whether it would be better dealt with privately; the relative importance of the problem to the individual and the group, compared with the value of the planned programme.

Make the decision and act on it without delay, before the meeting has moved irretrievably in a direction you have not chosen.

## Difficult questions

If questions arise which you cannot answer, do not try to bluff your way through. Admit your inadequacy and enquire first whether any other group member can throw any light on the subject.

If not, offer to find out for the next meeting, or ask other members to try to find out, or arrange to invite an expert in at a later date. It is sometimes helpful to wait until there are several such questions and to hold a special meeting to deal with them. If a Question Box is available at each meeting, it is easy to collect the questions.

## Arguments

There is room for genuine disagreement, but not for argument, in a group Bible study. If arguments do arise, try to let each side have its say and then firmly close the subject. If the participants wish to prolong their argument later, that is for them to decide, but they must not be allowed to break up the meeting.

## Troublemakers

Occasionally people may attend a meeting merely to cause trouble. This is more likely to happen with a younger group, and provided the leader is held in respect, he will be able to deal firmly with them.

If the leader is a contemporary, he will have more difficulty and should try to reason with the troublemakers in private rather than have a public show-down.

It is sometimes possible to employ troublemakers and so keep them out of mischief. For instance, they may be given the task of working the tape recorder, or assembling the visual aid. Provided they are in the limelight, they are often happy and will cease to cause trouble.

If nothing else works, you may have to exclude them from the meeting for the good of the group, but this must be a last resort.

# Time runs out

If the meeting does not follow the timetable you have planned and additional time is needed for one part of the meeting, it is best to omit one part and to close on time.

# Too many members

The optimum number for a group is a debatable point and it depends to some extent on its composition. In general, ten has been found to be a good number — there are sufficient people to afford variety but not too many to prevent all from expressing their thoughts. If a group of adults has more than twelve members, it is cumbersome and should be divided, either permanently or for a large part of each meeting.

# Too few members

What is the smallest viable group? Again, it depends to some extent on the people, but a satisfactory study can be held with only two or three people, provided each is willing and able to make some contribution to the discussion. There is no need to disband if numbers are low. Particularly when a group is being established, small numbers are helpful, enabling the group to be built up gradually and with the deep fellowship which is less easy to attain in a bigger group.

# Theme or book?

Some leaders strongly defend the idea of studying the Bible a book at a time, others feel equally strongly that it is best to study it not by book but by theme.

The Bible offers teaching on many themes, and it can be helpful to put together all the references to one theme in order to gain a composite view of the Biblical teaching on it. There are some dangers inherent in this system, but the leader who is aware of them will be more able to avoid them.

# Dangers of theme study

1   It is tempting to select only those passages which support our own opinions.

2   It is easy to take verses out of context and attach a wrong meaning to them.

3   It is easy to select a verse because of one word it contains and twist it to make it relevant to the theme.

4   A regular group may have a particular interest in one type of subject and may concentrate on that to the exclusion of others. This can cause unbalanced teaching.

5   If the theme is selected and Biblical passages are then sought to throw light on the subject, the passages selected may not deal specifically with the selected subject. An unsatisfactory study may follow in which the meaning of the passage is distorted or else the subject is modified.

It is helpful to find passages which deal not directly with the subject, but with the principles underlying it. For instance, if someone were to suggest a Bible study on strikes and trade unions, it could legitimately be protested that the Bible does not mention them, but a successful study could be held on personal relationships, work, those set in authority and our relationship with them, etc.

## Problems of the consecutive study of a book

1   It takes a long time to work through any book other than the shorter epistles and the minor prophets, and members – and leaders ! – tend to lose heart. Selections of a longer book can be studied to overcome this problem.

2   The books of the Bible were not written to be studied in a weekly meeting in small chunks, and they do not always lend themselves to suitable division. Care needs to be taken in selecting passages, and if a series of studies is planned, it is helpful to form a loose outline at the beginning so that sensible divisions are adopted.

In general there is much to commend the systematic study of a book :

1   It provides a balanced study including a range of topics.

2   It encourages members to consider what the passage says and to apply it as appropriate rather than to force an application to a pre-selected subject.

3   It obviates the necessity for constant selection of another subject.

4   It enables members easily to do some preparation for the following meeting.

As you can see, both these methods of Bible study have advantages and problems. If you have a regular group, vary the procedure you adopt. Section 3 of this book (page 133 and following) consists of a number of theme Bible study outlines and a verse by verse study on Paul's letter to the Colossians.

# SECTION 1 CONTENTS

## SIXTEEN METHODS OF GROUP BIBLE DISCUSSION

(Throughout this section, reference will be made to sample studies, using the various methods described. These are collected in Section 2.)

# METHOD

## QUESTION AND ANSWER

See samples 5 and 6 for the method in use.

## The method

The leader asks questions which are calculated to make the reader study the text before answering. This is the basic method for Group Bible study, on which there are many variations.

*Major variations on method*
1　Basic doctrines.
2　Key questions.
3　Three questions.

*Minor variations which can be incorporated into any major Q and A method*
1　Buzz groups. Divide the group into small groups of threes and fours to discuss a question before reporting back to the entire group.

All the buzz groups may discuss the same question, or each take a different one. The questions should be short and able to be answered quickly. Long or more complicated questions are more thoroughly grasped if they are written on a slip of paper for each group member. If a considerable time is allocated for group discussion, the written question will help to keep the group to the subject. Each small group appoints a member to report back to the entire group. With younger children, to obviate the necessity for oral reporting back, sheets of paper may be handed out, one to each group, on which they write their answers to written questions which circulate the groups, in the manner of a party game. Points may be allocated at the end for correct answers.

2　These groups all need capable leadership. Read to the group a passage of the Bible, or tell them certain facts from which they can deduce others, and then ask questions based on that information.

3　The questions and answers can be charted on a board or sheet of paper to be a record and reminder of the proceedings. (See also Method 11.)

# Points to note

1 The questions need to be thought out carefully. Vague or complicated questions produce a puzzled silence, and over-simplified ones an embarrassed silence, neither of which is conducive to free and lively discussion!

2 *Guiding principles in choice and delivery of questions*
   (1) Use words which can be understood at one hearing.
   (2) Pitch them at the right level – neither too difficult nor too easy for the majority.
   (3) Only ask questions to which you know at least one answer – otherwise you could be in a spot if a group member were to throw the question back at you!
   (4) Avoid a string of questions fired like shots from a pistol, as no one wants to feel like a sitting target, and short sharp questions have unfortunate associations with school tests.
   (5) Be prepared to repeat the question in several different ways and to keep talking gently until a spark of response appears in someone's eye.
   (6) Look at the group while you ask a question – they will not answer while you take refuge in your notes.
   (7) Try to be relaxed. This will help the group to be the same, and to answer naturally and freely – though beware that it does not induce sleep!
   (8) Do not ask a series of questions which require the answer 'yes' or 'no' as this will quickly kill any spark the meeting may have.
   (9) Listen to and acknowledge all answers, even if you disagree with them. A gentle remark such as, 'Yes, that's one way of looking at it, but don't you think that here it means . . . ?' helps to smooth away a wrong answer.
   (10) Be prepared to ask supplementary questions either to clarify the point made in the answer or to take it a stage further.
   (11) Speak confidently, but avoid giving the impression of being the fount of all knowledge, as this annoys the experienced members and inhibits the shy ones. It also demonstrates a lack of humility.

## Suitable groups

With modifications, any group can make use of this method. A group experienced at either private or group Bible study will need more coaxing than a well-established group of Christians, but with a competent leader the method can be effective in most situations.

# METHOD

## BASIC DOCTRINES

See also 'Points to note' on Method 1.

## The method

Many people find the following method useful for personal Bible study, but it can also be adapted for group use.

*Pray* before reading that God will help you to understand and receive His word.

*Read* carefully the Bible passage.

*Think* about what you have read, asking questions such as:

1 What is the passage basically about?
2 What does it teach about God the Father, His Son our Lord Jesus Christ, or the Holy Spirit?
3 What does it teach about Life?
   Is there a command, a promise, a warning? An example to follow or an error to avoid?

*Pray* after reading, using the thoughts you have gained as the basis for prayer.

The questions can be discussed immediately the passage has been read, or after a few minutes' silent study or quiet discussion with a neighbour.

## Suitable groups

Groups of any age — but preferably with some previous experience of Bible study — can make use of this method. It can be adopted by a group which has no experienced leader, as the questions are intrinsic to the method, and provided group members are sufficiently mature to agree when to move on to the next question, a satisfactory study can be held.

However, if there is an experienced leader he will be able to steer the discussion and summarize the findings, which makes for a better study.

# METHOD

# 3

## KEY QUESTIONS

See sample 4 for the method in use.

## The method

Read the passage several times and select the main points for consideration at the meeting. Work out questions which raise these points.

At the meeting, read the passage, then ask the key questions one at a time, or as appropriate, and give the group time to consider them by looking back at the passage. (The questions may be written on slips of paper.) Alternatively, give the questions before the passage is read, so that members can consider them during the reading of the passage. This helps them to concentrate while the passage is being read, and may save time. The kind of question which may be useful:

List the points about . . .

How many things does the passage say about . . . ?

What can we learn about the character of . . . ?

What reasons does the writer give for . . . ?

In our lives, what can we learn about . . . ?

The answers to these and similar questions will provide material for discussion of the main points of the passage.

See also 'Points to note' on Method 1.

## Suitable groups

Any group with even limited experience of Bible study can make use of this method. A good commentary (see Bibliography) will enable a relatively inexperienced leader to handle the method.

# METHOD

## THREE QUESTIONS

### The method

1 Read the passage.

2 Each person silently re-reads the passage and decides (1) the theme, (2) his favourite verse, and (3) the most difficult verse.

3 After all have made their selection, each in turn says what he thinks the theme is, and this is discussed; each explains which is his favourite verse and why, which may result in discussion; and which is his most difficult verse, after which other members offer help where possible.

### Points to note

1 An experienced leader is needed for this method. He needs to know how long to let each person speak, and when and how to stop him, or how to encourage him to say more. He should also be able to provide some explanation of all the verses in the passage in case satisfactory explanations are not offered by group members.

2 It is important not to miss the main point of the passage by dwelling on details. It may help if the leader summarizes the main points from time to time where appropriate.

### Suitable groups

Groups with some experience of Bible study will make good use of this method. They need not necessarily be experienced as a group, but should be sufficiently mature to give reasons for their choice of verse and be able to help each other with difficult verses. It is unlikely that younger members will find the method helpful.

# METHOD

**5** ?↓🕯

## SWEDISH METHOD

See sample 1 for the method in use.

## The method

1   Give each member a card divided into three sections, the first of which has the symbol of a question mark, the second an arrow, and the third a candle.

2   Read the Bible passage.

3   Allow the group ten minutes (or an appropriate length of time) to study the passage and to write comments on the cards. At the question mark, each person (or pair, if the members prefer to work in twos) notes any word, expression, or verse which is not understood. In the arrow section, he notes anything which he thinks should be acted upon.

4   Ask each person in turn to say what he has written in the question mark section. Discuss this, then adopt the same procedure with the arrow section.

5   Finally, either individually or as a group, members enter in the candle section anything which has become clear from their study of the passage.

6   Summarize.

7   If appropriate, close the meeting with open prayer based on what has been learned.

## Points to note

1   The leader needs to have the cards ready before the meeting begins.

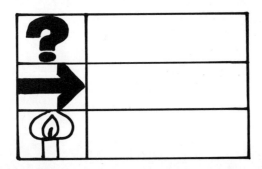

2  The leader needs to prepare the passage thoroughly and if necessary give an introduction to the passage and a few explanatory remarks.

3  Too much time must not be spent on any one section.

4  The leader's summary should be brief and should not repeat everything which has been said.

5  As a variation, the cards and instructions can be given out at the previous meeting so that the group assembles with their comments on sections 1 and 2 written in.

## Suitable groups

Any group may use this method, provided members are capable of working through a passage on their own and getting something out of it. Younger groups are less likely to benefit from it and groups with little knowledge of the Bible would probably not find it easy.

# METHOD

# 6

## DRAMATIZATION

See sample 7 for the method in use.

## The method

(If printed plays are being used, points 1–5 can be ignored.)

1 Study the Bible passage in detail, using any suitable method.

2 When group members are well acquainted with the content, allocate parts and give members a few minutes to consider the characters they each represent, entering as far as possible into their thoughts, feelings and attitudes.

3 Determine the general content of each scene. The narrator holds a key position and should give careful consideration to what he is to say, to give a confident and crisp framework to the whole.

4 Act out the incident, members extemporizing and reacting as they think the characters would have done. After a few trial runs an unwritten 'script' will evolve.

5 At this stage refer to the Bible passage again to ensure that there is nothing in the script which is inconsistent with it.

6 Present the drama. Opportunity should be given to non-performers to help in any way possible. An audience is not needed, and would in many cases be a hindrance to serious study.

7 The dramatization (whether printed or extemporized) can be followed by discussion which should raise the salient points of the passage. For instance, consideration may be given to the meaning of the incident, the change in attitude of any of the characters, the purpose behind the action, the message for us today, etc. Specific questions along these lines need to be prepared beforehand by the leader. In a large group, subdivision may be necessary for discussion, in which case each small group should have a competent leader furnished with written questions. Each group may consider a different aspect of the incident, and report back afterwards.

If the printed play is not very close to the Biblical account of the incident, the study time may be taken up with comparing the two and considering the implications of the Bible passage.

## Points to note

1 The drama may be of any length provided it does not become an end in itself, and sufficient time is allowed for study and discussion before or after the dramatic session.

2 There are several books of plays/playlets in print. (See list on p. 24 .)

23

3  Printed plays are not essential, and any Biblical incident can be dramatized by an enterprising group. With adult leadership, young people endowed with little academic ability can dramatize and extemporize effectively. Some years ago I steered a scarcely-literate 8th stream, secondary modern school group through the early chapters of Acts by reading aloud a section at a time and encouraging them to act it. This they did with considerable insight and enthusiasm, and it hardly mattered that Peter and John were arrested 'in the name of the sheriff of Nottingham'! After all, the basic ideas were right!

4  The preparation of the extempore drama (or the study of the printed play) ensures that the group consider in detail the text of the Bible passage, and this is the major aim.

It should be noted that the method is not to be adopted purely to entertain a group of bored youngsters, although the entertainment value is considerable, and use can rightly be made of it.

5  The final presentation may take the form of a play-reading (where all the characters sit in a circle) or an acted drama, with or without an audience.

## Suitable groups

Young people's groups find this a particularly satisfying way of studying the Bible, although there is no reason why older groups should not make use of it.

It is a useful method with which to introduce a group to Bible study. It is helpful if the members of the group already know each other, as they are then less likely to be inhibited. However, young people soon get used to the idea and lose their inhibitions!

## Printed playlets

*Gospel Dialogues* (selected chapters): Pickering and Inglis.

*A Man called Jesus* – Fontana – highly recommended for this use.

Chapter headings:

    1  The boyhood of Jesus
    2  The baptism of Jesus
    3  The temptation of Jesus
    4  The calling of the disciples
    5  The healing of the paralysed man
    6  The healing at the pool of Bethesda
    7  The healing of the man born blind
    8  Jesus returns to Galilee
    9  The Lord's prayer
  10  The Centurion's servant
  11  Christ the Son of God
  12  The Transfiguration
  13  The journey to Jerusalem
  14  The parable of the Pharisee and the tax-collector
  15  Christ enters Jerusalem

# METHOD

# 7

## INTERVIEW
## (WITH OR WITHOUT
## DRAMATIZATION)

See sample 7 for the method in use.

## The method

1   Read the passage. One person may read it or several may dramatize it (see Method 6).

2   Select an interviewer to prepare questions to be addressed to one or more of the characters involved. He may either project himself into the time of the action, and speak as if he were a contemporary reporter on, for instance, the 'Bethlehem Echo' or the 'Jericho Times' or he may act the part of a 20th century reporter whisked out of his century rather in the manner of 'Dr. Who'. In the latter case, the presentation may be done effectively as a television interview. His questions need to be selected and phrased carefully in order to elicit naturally and briefly as much information as possible from the interviewee.

3   Discuss together which character or characters in the story should be interviewed, and select group members to represent them.

4   Allow time for all the participants to become thoroughly acquainted with the passage.

5   If the interview is not to be conducted from a prepared script (and this would tend to give a rather stilted effect), the interviewer and interviewee should have an agreed plan for the direction the interview should take, and the points to be covered.

6   Hold the interview.

7   This may be followed by questions from the floor to probe further into the situation. In this case the interviewee needs to be fully conversant with the Bible passage and its context.

8   General discussion may follow, as in Method 6, point 7.

## Points to note

1   The aim is to make the incident comprehensible and memorable to the group, and to give them a deeper insight into its meaning and implications.

2   Passages should be chosen which give sufficient material for the answers of the interviewee to be based on the passage and not left purely to his imagination.

## Suitable groups

As in Method 6, except that younger children will probably find it too difficult; adult groups will probably be happier with this than with dramatization.

# METHOD

## DIALOGUE

See samples 6 and 8 for the method in use.

### The method

1 Read and study the passage.

Either 2 Split the group into pairs to hold discussions, one of them using the points made in the passage, the other arguing against him, using any arguments he can think of. Each pair then hold their dialogue before the whole group.

Or 3 Leader acts as 'devil's advocate' and puts forward various points of view which can be refuted by the members from the passage.

### Points to note

1 The real study of the passage comes in the marshalling of arguments and counter-arguments.

2 Care must be taken to make full use of the points in the passage, and not to allow members to diverge from it.

3 It may be helpful to conclude the study with a summary of the passage.

### Suitable groups

Older intelligent teenagers will find this stimulating, and those with little or no faith may be brought to realize the intellectual acceptability of the Christian creed, although experienced leaders will be needed in this case. Other groups will find that the use of the method encourages clear and deep thinking, and any except the youngest groups can make use of it.

# METHOD

## NEWSPAPER REPORT

See sample 9 for the method in practice.

## The method

In the simplest use of this method, the group compiles a report of a Biblical incident to be published in a contemporary newspaper. A more ambitious project is for the group to act as reporters, photographers (i.e. artists) and editors, and between them to compile an edition or editions of a newspaper. In the latter case, the same incident may be reported from various angles, and given editorial comment and 'photographs' (i.e. artists' impressions); or a number of incidents all relating to the same theme may be reported. Themes could include the plagues of the Egyptians and the events leading up to and including the escape of the Israelites, or incidents in the life of David, or St. Paul, or any other Biblical character whose life holds excitement, or the last days and death and resurrection of Jesus.

## Points to note

1  The project should be within the capabilities of the group. Even a simple and straightforward report takes a long time for a group to compile, and members will become disheartened if the project is not finished in the time available. On the other hand, if several meetings are allocated to the task, something more ambitious can be undertaken.

2  The incidents to be reported must be read and re-read, preferably in several different translations, to ensure familiarity, and the final report(s) compared with the Biblical account to eliminate discrepancy.

3  If one incident is to be reported by several different people, each from a specialized angle, the differing viewpoints must be carefully worked out (a) to ensure that each report is self-consistent, and (b) to prevent repetition in different articles.

4  Although it is often quicker for one person to prepare a report on his own, most groups will be happier working together and will gain from each other's ideas.

5  Artistic members of the group should be identified at the outset and given a suitable assignment.

6  There should be opportunity for the end-product to be displayed.

7  The leader should not be attached to a group, but should be

free to keep an eye on progress and to help where necessary to ensure that all groups finish at more or less the same time.

## Suitable groups

The method is especially suitable for groups of young people, and any group which likes activities.

If any groups feel the method is too juvenile for them, they could be asked to do it as an exhibit for younger people. For instance, a group of young wives who are not very experienced at Bible study could be asked to prepare a newspaper for a group of young people, and it could be a useful introduction to Bible study for both groups. Or a group of older teenagers could prepare it for younger ones, or for a local ESN school.

# METHOD

# 10

## CASE HISTORY OR TOPICAL STUDY

See sample 3 for the method in use.

## The method

1 Give a modern case history describing a problem situation from life. This may be taken from a newspaper, or your own experience, and could be a dilemma facing a business man, a discipline problem in a school, a difficult relationship between two people, a question of authority of a parent, friction in a church, etc.

2 Discuss with the group the solution to the problem. Comments may be written up on a chart.

3 Suggest a Bible passage or passages relating to the situation. Study this, then work out answers to the original problem, or the principles from which the answers may be deduced.

4 Write up these answers on the chart and compare them with the original ones.

## Points to note

1 Too much time should not be spent on stage one – the aim of this stage is to get the group thinking about the problem.

2 The leader should think carefully before selecting cases where the parties involved may be known to the group members.

3 The study of the Biblical passage(s) can be conducted in any appropriate way.

4 Care should be taken to establish the principles the Bible suggests and not to draw hasty conclusions on specific subjects.

## Suitable subjects and passages

| | |
|---|---|
| Work relationship – friction in the church – | 2 Thess. 3. 6–15 |
| | Matt. 25. 14–30 |
| | Philippians 2 |
| Temptation – how can I resist it? | Luke 4. 1–13 |
| Guidance – how can I be sure? | Psalm 25. 1–15 |
| | Acts 13. 1–3, 16. 6–10 |
| Husbands and wives – | Eph. 5. 21–33 |
| 'Unjust' suffering of a Christian | 1 Peter 3. 13–18, 4. 12–19 |
| Bad leaders | Ezekiel 34. 1–31 |
| Nominal faith | Jeremiah 7. 1–34 |
| Unfair dealings | Amos (selections) |

| Authority and discipline | Proverbs (selections) |
| Anger | Gen. 4. 1–16 |
| | John 2. 13–22 |
| | Eph. 4. 26–27 |
| Ambition | Matt. 20. 20–28 |
| | Romans 12. 3–13 |

## Suitable groups

This method can be used by any group capable of thinking through the implications of a situation, and working out basic principles. Older teenagers who are well-versed in the Bible may find that the use of this method helps them to relate Biblical teaching to everyday life. Equally, a group with little Biblical background may be surprised to find how relevant the Bible is to everyday problems, and may thus be encouraged to study it in more detail.

# METHOD

# 11

## AUDIO VISUAL AID
## PLUS BIBLE STUDY

## General points

There are two basic kinds of audio and visual aid – expensive and inexpensive.

A. *Expensive*

These include filmstrips, soundstrips (filmstrips with tape-recorded commentaries), tapes, records, slides and films. Many can be bought, borrowed or hired, and in some cases the group can make them for themselves.

For hiring, etc. see list at end of chapter.

B. *Inexpensive*

*Blackboard*

The use of this is not as easy as it appears, and needs practice.

*Whiteboard*

Shelf or ceiling paper at approx. 12½p per roll, which can be cut in pieces and fastened with a bulldog clip on to a board. Felt pens can be used to build up charts, diagrams, etc.

*Flannelgraph*

As a background you need a large piece of flannelette, felt or velvet. This gives the surface to which all your labels will stick when you place them on the board. The pictures or labels can be backed with lint, wynceyette or flannelette. The pictures are stuck on the material, and when the paste is dry, the picture and the backing are trimmed together. (If the backing material is new, it should be washed and shrunk before pasting, as the water from the paste shrinks the material and so buckles the picture.) The pieces can be used again, and can be given a new lease of life by being pressed with a warm iron. Alternatively blotting paper may be used as a backing, or on its own, as you can write or draw on it with a felt-tip, spirit-ink pen. To make sure that it sticks to the flannelboard, roughen the back of the blotting paper with a wire brush or sandpaper, and tilt the board slightly backwards.

*Pictures and maps* – can be acquired from travel agents, cinemas, magazines, colour supplements, etc.

*The advantages of using AVA*

Audio or visual aids, however simple, can assist a Bible study group. They:

  A.  Help concentration.

  B.  Clarify meaning.

  C.  Aid the memory.

  D.  Obviate the necessity for lengthy oral explanation.

E. Are expected in a television age.
F. Offer variety in presentation.
G. Can be a reminder and record of the group's findings.

*The dangers of AVA*
A. Poor aids are worse than none at all.
B. They may stunt the imagination.
C. They may block the understanding of spiritual truth by representing it in a visual way.
D. They may be merely a gimmick, adding nothing to the value of the meeting.
E. A 'good' (i.e. attractive, well-presented) visual aid may distract attention from the point.
   If the leader is aware of these dangers, he is less likely to fall into them.

## Points to note

1 If a visual is hired, it is helpful to hear or view it before ordering, but this is not always possible. If on arrival, the aid proves to be unsuitable, the temptation to use it should be resisted, unless it can be adapted to make it suitable.

2 The leader should try out the aid and become familiar with it before the meeting, and prepare any charts, questions, etc. which are necessary.

3 Equipment and power points should be checked before the meeting and all aids tried out for audibility, visibility, etc. in the meeting room.

4 AVA are *aids* and do not offer an easy way for a lazy leader to avoid preparation for group Bible study. As much, if not more, preparation needs to go into the meeting if AVA are used.

*Basic uses of Audio and Visual Aids with Bible study*
1 To introduce the subject matter.
2 To illustrate the points as they arise.
3 To summarize the findings of the group.
4 To stimulate discussion and further the study of Biblical teaching on points made, e.g. in the tape or filmstrip.

1 *To introduce the subject matter of a Bible study*
Audio and visual aids here can range from the very simple use of a picture to the sophisticated use of a film.

*Examples of the use of simple visual aids*
*Any Christian Aid poster*, plus a Bible study on suffering, using 1 Peter 2. 18–25; 3. 13–18; 4. 12–19.

*A picture of an empty church*, followed by a study on 'What is the Church?' using Acts 2. 37–47; 4. 32–37; 5. 1–12.

Many pictures can be used in this way and a leader will do well to collect anything which at some time come in useful.

*Examples of the use of sophisticated visual aids*
*Films* are of limited usefulness here because the complications of projection are such that it is hardly worth while as a mere introduction to a meeting.

There are many tapes, filmstrips and soundstrips which are excellent for the purpose and have the advantage of being easy to use.

*Tapes.* 'We've got an excuse and we're sticking to it' (Scripture Union) in which Cindy Kent and Cliff Richard talk about how and why they read the Bible (running time 13½ minutes). This could be followed by a study on what the Bible claims to be and how it can be used. The following passages would be suitable:

Psalm 119 (esp. 1- 40). Learning God's plan for living.

Luke 24. 25–27; Matt. 12. 3, 5; 19. 4; 21. 16, 42; 22. 31. Attitude of Jesus to the Old Testament.

2 Tim. 2. 15. The use of Scripture.

2 Tim. 3. 14–17. What the Scriptures can do for a person.

2 Peter 3. 15–16. Wrong use of Scripture.

Tapes can be made by the group members, or by the leader and other helpers:

e.g. Tape and edit the communion services of different denominations (preferably from the radio) and play them back at the meeting before holding a Bible study on 1 Cor. 11. 23–32 and Matt. 26. 26–29;

or Make up and tape a playlet depicting quarrelling in the church, to be played to the group before consideration of 1 Cor. 3;

or Make up and tape a playlet about different attitudes to culture, fashion, leisure activities, etc. to be followed by a study of 1 Cor. 6. 12–20; 1 Cor. 8 and 1 Cor. 10. 23–33.

*Filmstrips* with a printed commentary to be read aloud (or pre-recorded and played in the manner of a soundstrip).

*The Psalms of David* (Carwal Ltd.) followed by a study of Psalm 23 and 121, or the parable of the lost sheep (Luke 15. 3–7), or Jesus as the Good Shepherd (John 10. 1–18).

*Survey of the Scriptures* (Fact and Faith Filmstrip) – 10 strips each introducing a different section of the Bible – £1.25 each strip.

Six filmstrips on Christian beginnings, belief and behaviour (Church Pastoral-Aid Society). These are made by an Anglican society and called 'Your Confirmation' but may be used effectively by any denomination. Christian Belief Part 2 could be followed by a study from the gospels on aspects of the Person and Work of Christ.

Six strips called *In Our Stead* and six called *Words from the Cross* (Concordia): 30p to hire, £1.50 to buy per strip, designed to show parallels between the situations Jesus faced and people's reactions then and now. These could be followed by study of sections of the gospels.

*Soundstrips* (filmstrips with a tape-recorded commentary).

*Number One* (Scripture Union) lasts 17 minutes. This is the story of Joe, who from babyhood thinks he is the centre of the world and everything is for him – until he is confronted by Jesus Christ. This is a humorous and positive cartoon strip which can be hired, together with specially written discussion material.

*The Rise and Fall of Sir Ivor Lott* (Scripture Union) lasts 7 minutes. An amusing cartoon strip which could be followed by studies on many subjects, e.g.

> Ambition, using 3 John 1–11 ; Romans 12. 3–13 ; Matt. 20. 20–28.

> Self-centredness and relationships are two other possible themes.

*Hitting It Off* (Scripture Union) has three sections, each lasting five minutes, dealing with relationships at work, with parents, and with friends. Each section should be used on its own, and could be followed by a study on relationships, using, e.g. Philippians 2 or on obedience, work, priorities, etc.

### 2 *To illustrate the points as they arise*

*Flannelgraph* is useful here, and can be used effectively with any age, although it is usually reserved for younger people (under 14). Flash cards (card with one word or phrase written on) may be used to draw attention to the point being made in the passage, e.g. in Ephesians 1. 3–10 in a consideration of the question 'What has God done?' flash cards with the words 'blessed', 'chosen', 'destined', 'bestowed', 'made known' may be put on to the flannelgraph as each word is mentioned. This method serves also to summarize the findings of the group.

(*a*) Pictures of the participants in a dramatic incident may be moved around the flannelgraph to show the development of the story, e.g. parable of the Good Samaritan (Luke 10. 29–37) ; parable of the Prodigal Son (Luke 15. 11–32), the incident on the Emmaus Road (Luke 24. 13–35).

(*b*) A diagram may be built up gradually to illustrate the points as they emerge, e.g. the sequence in the Creation story (Gen. 1), with pictures to represent each aspect of the Creation. Or, in studying a Biblical character, e.g. Daniel, pictures or labels may be placed around a central figure to represent the influences at work for and against him, as the book is studied.

*Maps* can be useful to show where the action takes place, e.g. the missionary journeys of St. Paul, the movements of Jesus, or the geographical situation of the enemies of Israel, or Palestine's position in the Roman Empire, etc.

*A blackboard or a whiteboard* can be used in a similar way to the flannelgraph, except that figures can only accumulate and cannot be moved. A sequence can be depicted by using a series of sheets of white paper.

*Hand and finger puppets* may be used with young children to illustrate the events in the passage being studied. These can be made, or purchased from Gospel Light. (Kit of Selected Biblical Characters, price 81p.)

*Tapes* can be used to illustrate points as they arise. For instance, a Bible passage can be read and a prepared tape depicting a modern situation can be played to illustrate the principle outlined in the passage. The passage can then be studied in detail. Many sections from the epistles or sections of the Sermon on the Mount (Matt. 5–7) lend themselves to this – e.g. using Matt. 7. 3–5 a tape can be played of a self-righteous person criticizing another for something of which he himself is more guilty.

*Filmstrips* may be used provided too great an upheaval is not necessary in changing from viewing to discussion.

*Amos the Prophet* (Carwal £1.50) has six parts. These include sections on the youth of Amos, the contemporary social and political scene, and three sections dealing with the visions of Amos, his mission and message and his banishment.

*The Life of Paul* (Carwal £1.37½) is divided into seven sections for group study, and has notes at both adult and junior levels.

*Temptation* (Church Army £1.50) shows the temptations of Jesus, Luke 4. 1–13, and man's reaction to equivalent temptations, with examples from Old and New Testaments.

### 3. *To summarize the findings of the group*

Many of the charts, etc. suggested under 2 ('To illustrate the points as they arise') can be of use here as well, and can remain on display as a reminder and record after the meeting has ended. Lists may be written up (on board, etc.) of what has been learned – e.g. the key word from each verse, the characteristics of the people in the story, etc. A prepared table may be filled in.

Many filmstrips offer an excellent summary of books or passages studied, and can be a useful conclusion to a meeting or series, e.g.

*Our Old Testament Heritage* (Church Army £1.37½) – a comprehensive appraisal of Abraham, Moses, Amos, Jeremiah and Habakkuk.

*Women of the Old Testament* (Church Army £1.12½ per strip) – two strips depicting approx. forty women.

*Parables of the Kingdom* (Church Army £1.12½) – seven parables from Matt. 13.

### 4. *To stimulate discussion and further study of Biblical material*

*Filmstrips*. Many are available. The leader should be familiar with the strip before the meeting, and preferably have notes or a script, as it is difficult to recall the exact subject-matter after one viewing. It may be helpful to stop at intervals and discuss what has been said, and look up the Biblical references. Members of the group will probably gain more from this if they read the relevant passages before the meeting.

*Spokesmen for God* (Carwal £1.37½) – depicts Elijah pleading for the worship of the true God against a background of blatant idolatry; Micah denouncing man's greed and selfishness and demanding justice, mercy and loving kindness; and Haggai reminding the Jews of their indebtedness to God. Suitable for an older group, experienced at Bible study, and familiar with the content of the prophetic books.

*The Life of Christ* (Carwal £1.12½ each of the two parts),

followed by detailed study of some of the incidents portrayed.

*Peter and Cornelius* (Carwal 37½p), followed by a discussion on intolerance, based on the teaching of Acts 10.

# Bibliography for Method 11

*References in text*

Concordia, 117 Golden Lane, London, E.C.1.

Christian Aid, 10 Eaton Gate, London, S.W.1.

Scripture Union (AVA loans), 5 Wigmore Street, London, W1H 0AD (for loan or sale).

Carwal Ltd., 85 Manor Road, Wallington, Surrey (for hire or sale).

Fact and Faith Films, Falcon Court, 32 Fleet Street, London, E.C.4 (for sale).

Church Pastoral-Aid Society, Falcon Court, 32 Fleet Street, London, E.C.4 (for sale).

Gospel Light, Bush House, 4th Floor, NE Wing, Aldwych, London, W.C.2.

*Other distributors of filmstrips*

Church Army, 185 Marylebone Lane, London, N.W.1. (sale and hire – comprehensive catalogue).

SPCK, Holy Trinity Church, Marylebone Road, London, N.W.1 (sale and hire).

Religious Films Ltd., 6 Eaton Gate, London, S.W.1 (sale and hire).

Keswick Tapes.

Many organizations produce filmstrips, but the above is a comprehensive list of places from which most of these can be acquired. Most organizations have facilities for viewing on approval. Order well in advance to avoid disappointment.

# METHOD

# 12

## CHARACTER STUDY

See samples 2 and 3 for the method in practice.

## Method

1  Read the relevant passage.

2  Enumerate the main points of the incident. If the group is inexperienced, the leader should do this in order to save time and move quickly on to the main part of the study.

3  Ask the group members to suggest as many points as possible about the character of the person under discussion, and to say from which verses they have made their deductions. Initially, this may be done in twos or by individuals jotting down their thoughts on paper before reporting to the whole group. By this method the character of the person is gradually built up.

The leader should ask for amplification or further evidence from the passage, and keep a record – on a piece of paper or a chart – of the findings.

4  Discuss each point, with application where possible.

5  Summarize orally or on a chart.

## Points to note

1  The leader should ensure that the passage is studied in detail.

2  Evidence for each point should be produced from the text, and no unfounded ideas allowed to pass unquestioned.

3  If the study is based on several extracts from the Bible, it will be helpful if all members of the group have read the relevant passages before the meeting.

4  If this is impracticable, the passage may be first summarized by the leader, and then studied in depth by small groups each taking a section and reporting to the others.

5  The members may be divided into small groups, each to study a particular character in the story.

## Suitable groups

An experienced leader with an inexperienced group could make good use of this method. People of any age will enjoy it and find it worthwhile. It is particularly useful for introducing young people to Bible study. A young wives' group with little Biblical background could study women of the Bible to demonstrate the relevance of Bible study to life today.

# Passages suitable for use with this method

*Longer passages* (to be read before the meeting or studied in sections by small groups). Ruth (The book of Ruth) ; Esther (The book of Esther) ; Hezekiah (2 Kings 18–19) ; Joseph (Gen. 37–48) ; Peter (selections from Gospels and Acts).

*Shorter passages.* Rahab (Joshua 2) ; Gideon (Judges 6–8) ; David v. Goliath (1 Sam. 17. 12–54) ; Jesus in story of woman at the well (John 4. 1–42) ; Householder, tenants and son in parable of ungrateful tenants (Matt. 21. 33–43).

# METHOD

# 13

# COMMENTS

## The method

1   Spend a few minutes in silent study of the passage, or have members read it before the meeting.

2   Comment on each verse or group of verses in turn. For this, the leader may call upon a member to comment, or else members may volunteer.

3   Summarize the main points.

## Points to note

The leader needs to ensure that
- (a) one member of the group does not dominate and overawe the others, and
- (b) the comments are not too lengthy, with the verses merely an excuse for individuals to get on to their hobby horses.

## Suitable groups

Only a very experienced group can cope with this method, but with such a group it can be very effective if members are humble and prepared to listen to each other.

# METHOD

# 14.20

## TWENTY QUESTIONS

## Method

The basic idea is that the members of the group work out a series of twenty questions on a given passage, to be answered by the leader.

1   Divide the whole group into smaller groups and all study a prescribed passage, each group providing a few questions towards the twenty.

2   Members put their questions to the leader for his comments and answers.

3   General discussion may follow.

Alternatively, each group in turn can offer answers to another group's questions, after having been given time to study the passage and work out the answers.

## Points to note

1   The group members need to be fairly mature in order to select worthwhile questions.

2   The leader needs to be very familiar with the passage being studied, competent at answering questions, and well-versed in the Bible.

3   The questions may need some reorganization to give a sensible sequence. With some passages, each group could be given a separate section on which to ask questions, and the sections could then be dealt with in order by the leader.

## Suitable groups

This is a useful method for older teenagers who are new to Christianity. People tend to remember answers to questions they have asked more easily than they remember unsolicited information. A regular Bible study group may be able to invite a Biblical scholar to answer questions on a passage they have found difficult.

# METHOD

## BIBLE
## TEAM
## GAMES

There are many games which can be used with younger children – and sometimes with older ones – to make Bible study more exciting. Readers are recommended to see the booklet *40 Bible Games and Quizzes* published by Scripture Union in Scotland.

Some Bible games are purely a test of the knowledge the group members have already acquired and these have their place. Games which in themselves provide Biblical teaching have a more obvious use. Here are descriptions of three games:

(a) Word race

Divide the group into two teams. Place them at equal distances from a table on which are cards containing key words from the passage, one set of cards for each group. At a given signal, one member from each group collects a card, and on his return to the group a second member collects another until all cards have gone. The first team to arrange their cards in the order in which they occur in the Bible passage is the winner.

See sample 8 for method (a) in practice.

(b) Who am I?

Tell the group you are a Bible character and give them a clue as to your identity. Points are awarded according to how many or how few clues are needed before a member names the character.

(c) Find the verse

Take a passage and let members look it up in their Bibles. Read selected verses from the passage in various translations and award a point to the first one to identify the verse.

# METHOD

## 16

### GROUP PREPARATION

### Points to note

1    Although this may not seem to be a method, in practice it makes such a difference to the conduct of a Bible study that it can reasonably be classed as such.

2    There is no point in suggesting that members of a group prepare beforehand without giving clear details of exactly what is to be prepared and how: a vague suggestion that 'people might like to look at it before next week' is unlikely to produce much response. It is useful to provide questions based on a specific passage as this helps members to read the passage thoughtfully, and the answers to the questions give a starting point for the meeting itself. Advance preparation by the leader is necessary so that he can give instructions as to the preparation required.

3    If the leader asks the group to come prepared in some way, he should conduct the meeting on the assumption that the preparation has been done — nothing is more depressing than to have one's homework ignored! If, after a few attempts to use this method, it appears that the group are not able to prepare before the meeting, the method should be abandoned, as it cannot be successful if only a percentage have done the preparation.

4    It is preferable to work on a series of meetings based on a theme, so that the members become familiar with the theme, and the subject-matter is already in their minds when they begin their preparation for any given meeting. It is always easier to continue thinking about a subject at home on one's own than to start from scratch.

### Method

1    At the first meeting of the series, introduce the subject and do a basic introductory Bible study, without previous preparation on the part of the group.

2    Outline the subject-matter of the subsequent meetings and provide details of preparation to be done before the next meeting.

The preparation may involve

(1) detailed study of the text, in which case the next meeting should be conducted on the assumption that people are familiar with the content, and could take the form of a discussion from points raised;

or (2) wide reading of the context of the passage to be studied in detail at the meeting;

or (3) the consideration of general questions without Biblical references, in which case the meeting will consist of general discussion, followed by relevant Bible study (see Method 10) ;

or (4) different assignments may be given to each member, so that each comes to the meeting prepared to introduce one aspect of the subject or one section of the Bible passage.

## Suitable groups

This method is suitable only for use by a group experienced in Bible study, where members are willing and able to prepare beforehand. It is not suitable for a group which needs coaxing to study the Bible.

# SECTION 2 CONTENTS
## SAMPLE GROUPS IN ACTION

# PREFACE TO SAMPLES

The following series of nine samples or playlets has been prepared in order to illustrate several of the methods outlined in Section 1, and to demonstrate some of the good and bad techniques commonly adopted by leaders.

The left-hand page in each sample is an account of what took place at the meeting, and the right-hand page is a commentary on it. The two should be read in conjunction, and for the convenience of the reader, the numbers opposite the comments on the right-hand page correspond with the numbers opposite the contributions they relate to on the left-hand page.

I apologize if many of the comments seem too obvious, over-critical or misplaced. However, even the obvious comments may be of some help to the beginner. I have myself made many of the mistakes made by the leaders in the samples; this makes me a little less diffident at criticizing fictional characters. Nor do I claim omniscience on the subject, and some leaders may well disagree with my comments.

# INTERDENOMINATIONAL STUDY GROUP
## Members

| | |
|---|---|
| MR. AND MRS. MONTROSE | (see also sample 2) *aged 50; regular churchgoers.* |
| MR. AND MRS. SMITHSON | (see also sample 2) *recently started attending church with teenage children.* |
| MRS. MONTGOMERY | (see also sample 3) *aged 25; over-zealous in her approach to non-Christians.* |
| MR. PETERS | (see also sample 4) *elderly, rather negative in outlook.* |
| MRS. PETERS | (see also sample 4) *sweet, kind, and shockable.* |
| MISS GRIFFITHS | (see also sample 4) *mid 20's; teacher; well-versed in Biblical matters.* |
| MRS. BANKS | *aged 30; quiet and shy.* |
| MRS. EVANS | *retired nurse; devout Christian; inclined to make lengthy irrelevant remarks.* |
| MR. WARNER | *retired teacher; tolerant of all viewpoints.* |

## Details

The local churches have arranged a series of meetings on selected chapters of John's gospel. There are several house groups and the members of each are from different denominations, but the same geographical area. The leadership rotates, and it is Miss Griffiths' turn this week.

1  MISS GRIFFITHS  Thank you all for coming again. You will remember that we are going to look at John 15, verses 1–17 today. Mr. Warner is going to open in prayer.

2  MR. WARNER  We thank you, O Lord, for bringing us here together once more from all our different denominations. We thank you that we are able to meet together in this way, even though we are all from different denominations. Help us to understand each other better so that all the different denominations may feel united. Through Jesus Christ our Lord, Amen.

3  MISS G  Thank you, Mr. Warner. There are several New English Bibles here and if anyone hasn't one, please take one.

4  MR. PETERS (gruffly)  I'll stick to my Authorized Version. I don't hold with these modern translations. Can't see why they are needed. Nothing wrong with the AV. They get it all wrong in these modern ones, and they lose all the beauty and majesty. I don't hold with it.

# INTERDENOMINATIONAL STUDY GROUP

Sample 1

## METHOD

### SWEDISH

There is no delay and Miss Griffiths plunges straight into the meeting. This is good, as much time can be lost on unnecessary preamble, which can be frustrating and annoying to busy people. On the other hand, if a group is newly-formed and the members are not all well-acquainted with each other, it can be valuable to spend some time at the outset in general discussion. Our present group is quite well-established by now and its time is best spent in getting on with the job in hand.

Miss Griffiths has already asked Mr. Warner to open in prayer. This is more polite than calling upon a person at the last moment, and indicates to others that they need not fear an unexpected prayer being demanded of them.

3  It is useful to come prepared with spare Bibles, and Miss G wisely decides to avoid confusion by ensuring that all members have access to the same version.

4  A difficult customer who will need careful handling.

5     MISS G   The AV might be all right for those who are familiar with it, Mr. Peters, but I think it's difficult to understand, and I think it's silly to stick to it when there are better translations available. Personally I like the Revised Standard Version best, but as most people seem to have an NEB, it seemed a good idea to collect a few copies of that so that we could all follow it in the same translation. I think it's easier if we all use one translation as common ground, but then we can each have our favourite version as well. So you keep an eye on the AV for us, Mr. Peters, and tell us when it puts something particularly well, and we'll each make contributions from the various translations we have.

5b    I see you have Today's English Version, Mr. and Mrs. Smithson.

6     MR. SMITHSON   Yes, the kids bought us it and we read it most nights.

7     MISS G   Yours is the RSV, Mrs. Evans, and you have Moffatt, Mr. Warner. That's a good selection then.

7b    I have a tape of the passage we are going to look at, being read by a friend of mine who is training to be an actor. He is an enthusiastic Christian and I think you will find the way he reads it very helpful. He used the NEB.
(The tape is played.)

8     MRS. BANKS   That's marvellous! I've got a lot more out of it than I did when I read it at home on my own.

9     MRS. PETERS   I liked it too, He has such a lovely voice.

10    MRS. EVANS   He really meant it, didn't he? There are some people on TV who pretend to be Christians but you can tell they are just acting. I think there is a lot wrong with the religious programmes. They are far too wishy-washy, if you know what I mean. The other night I was watching . . .

11    MRS. MONTGOMERY   Some of them are awful, but they aren't all! There was a gospel service on the other evening, with some of Billy Graham's team, and some really good music. That was excellent and I'm sure it must have done a lot of good.

12    MR. PETERS   Filth, all filth, TV.

13    MRS. PETERS   Oh, come now dear, you know you like watching the religious programmes, and you always enjoy the children's programmes.

14    MR. WARNER   I think we are wandering a bit from the point. What are those cards in your hand, Miss Griffiths? Do you want them passing round?

15    MRS. PETERS (anxiously)   Is it a kind of party game, dear? Do you think we should, at a Bible study?

16    MISS G (laughing)   Well, you could call it a party game, Mrs. Peters, but when you see what it is, I'm sure you will be quite happy about it! We are going to use the Swedish Method today, so I would like you each to have one of these cards.

5          Miss Griffiths is unwise to criticize Mr. Peters so scathingly, but finally redeems the situation by acknowledging that he may have a contribution to make with his AV. Tact, particularly in those who are younger than the average in the group, is an essential attribute in a group leader.

5b–7a      It is useful to identify at the outset the various translations in use. A leader who has done adequate preparation will then be able to call upon individuals to read a particularly helpful verse in their own version. This helps to clarify the more obscure points, and on occasion gives the leader the opportunity to call upon one of the quieter members to make a simple contribution to the meeting.

7b         The pre-recording and playing of a tape of the passage being well read is helpful and less distracting than having the passage read badly by members who are concerned about where their own verse starts, and who have not had time to digest its meaning.

8–14       Much of this is irrelevant. The situation is retrieved by one of the members gently leading the leader! Miss G is failing in one of the leader's tasks, which is to keep the group members on the subject.

15–18      Miss G maintains her sense of humour (16) (a useful attribute for a leader) and her tact (18). She heads off the Common Market red herring and briefly and clearly explains what is required in the method to be used.

17  MR. P  Swedish Method! Don't know why they can't stick to good old English methods. No reason to use this imported stuff. I expect it's all to do with the Common Market.

18  MISS G  Well, no it isn't really, Mr. Peters! Now that everyone has a card, we'll have a look at them. You will see that there are three columns, each with a symbol at the left hand side. The first symbol is a question mark, and the idea is that we each study the passage for a while and jot down any words or ideas we do not fully understand. In the second section, where there is an arrow, we note any verses or ideas which should be acted upon. After that we will discuss the two sections and finally jot down in the last section, by the candle, anything that has become clear as a result of our study.

19  MR. MONTROSE  That's a novel idea. You mean we all sort of do our homework and then compare ideas?

20  MISS G  Yes, that's the idea. You might prefer to work on your own, or with someone else.

21  MRS. EVANS  I always prefer doing the thinking on my own because there aren't any distractions. I always get a great deal more out of a passage if I study it in silence. I remember once when . . .

22  MISS G (laughing)  Come on, Mrs. Evans, or else we will run out of time to compare our answers.

23  MR. PETERS (sullenly)  What do you want us to do, then?

24  MRS. PETERS  We've to write things down in these columns, haven't we, dear?

25  MISS G  Yes, but look back over the passage first and then if there are any points you are uncertain about, note them down by that question mark there, do you see? And then when you come across something that calls for action, or a response, note it down here, by the arrow.

26  MRS. PETERS  Thank you, dear. Do you want us to do it now?

27  MISS G  Yes please. It might take us ten or fifteen minutes. Most people are doing it in twos, aren't they? Except Mr. Warner and Mrs. Evans –
(All start reading and filling in cards.)

28  MR. SMITHSON  This is tremendous stuff, you know. We never realized what an interesting book the Bible was, did we, June? There are a few things here I don't understand, though. What's all this about fruit?

29  MRS. MONTGOMERY (mysteriously)  Ah, well, that's the fruit of the Spirit, and that only comes when you are a Christian.

30  MR. S  But what sort of fruit is it? Seems a funny idea to me.

31  MISS G  That is perhaps something we can discuss all together when we have all listed our queries. Have you

19–22    Reminiscences are pleasantly cut short, leaving no bad feelings. A pleasant manner can be most effective in bringing members to heel!

23–27    Patience in explaining a new technique is important, especially with older members – and often younger members, too – who do not naturally take to new methods. Repetition and the opportunity to ask questions are of great value. Flexibility is a help, allowing the members in this case to choose whether to work alone or in pairs. It is vital to stipulate at the outset the time allocated to an assignment, or else members have no idea how fast to work or how deeply to explore each point.

28–32    In a voluntary Bible study group, interruptions cannot be summarily squashed, and Miss G wisely does not attempt to impose the discipline of silence. A relaxed atmosphere such as is found in this group is more appropriate to the situation even though it may tend to slow down the progress. Miss G tactfully directs Mr. S back to the task in hand and sensibly gives an assurance that his problems will be dealt with in due course.

written it down as one of your queries?

32 MR. S  No, not yet. We were just getting the passage read. (Silence again, followed by a murmured discussion for a few minutes.)

33 MR. MONTROSE  I once heard a sermon on this passage. The preacher was saying that people who used to go to church and stopped going are the ones who will wither and be thrown on the fire. Quite right, too. They have no business to stop going to church. How do they think we're going to make ends meet? It costs just as much to run the place whether they are there or not. But they expect the church to be available if they want to be married or buried or anything. Our collections are down 50 per cent during the last two years, and the expenses are up by about 30 per cent. I was only saying to my wife the other day . . .

34 MRS. MONTGOMERY (severely)  It's not just the people who don't go to church, Mr. Montrose. There are plenty of people who do go to church who have not been converted – there are enough clergy not converted to cause us real concern. The ones who are going to be thrown into the fire are the ones who do not know Jesus Christ as their Lord and Saviour.

35 MR. MONTROSE  Well. of course, it all depends what you mean by converted. I don't really believe in it myself. Good-living people who go to church do not need to be converted in my opinion.

36 MRS. MONTGOMERY  Oh, I disagree with you completely on that. Conversion is absolutely vital. It doesn't have to be dramatic and sudden, you know, Mr. Montrose, though personally I think it is always better if it is sudden, because then you are quite sure that it has happened!

37 MISS G  Surely it doesn't matter how you are converted, so long as you are, Mrs. Montgomery? No one way is better than another, is it?

38 MRS. PETERS  I agree with you, dear. We are all good in our different ways.

39 MRS. MONTGOMERY (becoming agitated)  That's true, but it's not the same thing as becoming a Christian, Mrs. Peters. We all need to be converted, and it doesn't matter whether we are good or not.

40 MR. PETERS  Of course it matters whether we are good or not! That's the trouble with young people today – no standards.

41 MRS. MONTGOMERY  I didn't mean it doesn't matter whether we are good or not.

42 MR. P  That's what you said.

43 MRS. M  What I meant was that we need to become Christians even if we are relatively good people.

44 MR. MONTROSE (pompously)  Some of us don't need to *become* Christians. We go to church every Sunday and

33–46 A giant red herring! Miss G not only allows this to develop, but joins in (37). Conversion is an important subject, but her policy in 31 would have been appropriate again here, and she could have ensured that the subject was raised later in the full meeting. Once more Mr. W calls the meeting to order.

If a topic is raised which is a side issue to the main purpose of the meeting, one of a number of things may happen, and it is the leader's job to decide which is appropriate to his situation.

1 The subject may be discussed in full at that point. This may be desirable if a member is particularly troubled by it and needs help. However, if this occurs frequently, it tends to give a rather aimless and rambling atmosphere which can stunt clear thinking.

2 The subject may be held in abeyance until the main part of the meeting has been completed. The danger here is that no time will be left for it.

3 If the subject is a large one, it may be noted and raised at a subsequent meeting called specially for the purpose. Or a meeting may be arranged to tie up several loose ends from previous studies.

4 The subject may be promptly squashed and not raised again. This is appropriate only in exceptional circumstances, e.g. if the subject is raised merely to cause a diversion.

In the situation under consideration, Miss G allowed a few members to drift into the discussion. She should have either held up the meeting in order to hold a full discussion on the subject, or else arranged to raise it later.

never do anyone any harm. I am on three committees and I attend several meetings during the week.

45    MRS. M   But that doesn't make you a Christian.

45a   MR. M   Of course it does!

46    MR. WARNER   You people must all have finished your cards now, haven't you? I'm still working out what to put. (General chorus of 'No, not yet.' 'We need a few more minutes.' 'I was listening to the discussion.' 'I had forgotten about the cards.')

47    MISS G   Let's have two or three more minutes then, to fill in the first two sections. That is, points we do not understand, and those which call for action or response.

48    MRS. EVANS   I've done the third one as well, because I have already learned a great deal from the passage.

49    MISS G   Oh - er - well - er - I suppose that is all right. You were meant to do it later.
Is everyone just about ready now?
Never mind if you are not quite ready. We'll hear what you have put down and between us we will probably have covered all the main points.

50    MRS. P   We haven't written very much, I'm afraid, dear.

51    MISS G   If we each contribute one point, that should keep us going for a while, Mrs. P. Would you like to tell us one thing you have written in the question mark column?

52    MRS. P   It's in verse 5 – 'Apart from Me, you can do nothing.' We wondered if it was literally true, or what it means.

53    MISS G (briskly)   I think that as Jesus is talking in this passage about bearing fruit, He means we can't bear any fruit without Him. Do you agree?

54    MRS. P (in a puzzled voice)   Yes, dear. Thank you.

55    MISS G (briskly)   What is your first question, Mr. Smithson?

56    MR. S   It's what this fruit is. I don't seem to have got the hang of it yet.

57    MISS G   It's the fruit of the Spirit, you see.

58    MR. S   No, I don't see at all.

59    MR. WARNER   It's an analogy, isn't it? The idea is that we are like branches of a tree in that we need to be attached to the trunk of the tree, which is Jesus Christ. The so-called 'fruit' we can have is doing the things Christ wants us to do. We can't do these things without His strength, which is like sap flowing into us.

60    MR. S   Oh, I see. That makes more sense, thank you.

61    MRS. BANKS   Thank you, I begin to understand that now. I was always a bit hazy about it.

62    MRS. MONTGOMERY   It's like in Galatians 5, verses 22 and 23, isn't it?
(Pause.)

63    MISS G (with a slight twinkle)   Could you remind us of those verses, please, Mrs. Montgomery?

| 47 | A recapitulation of what is, or should be, being done, is useful at this point. |
| 48–49 | Miss G temporarily loses her tact and may make Mrs. E feel a little uncomfortable. |

Neither does she allow the promised two or three minutes for completion of the task. Unless everyone has completed the assignment, it is better to allow time that has been promised as conscientious members will have budgeted for it.

| 50–55 | The meeting is suddenly gathering speed! Has Miss G realized that too much time has elapsed? |

Even if time is short, it is normally better to encourage group members to answer and discuss each other's questions rather than to provide an immediate and succinct explanation oneself. Poor Mrs. P is a bit overwhelmed by the immediate and high-powered answer and is probably no nearer to understanding the point.

The next question is called for before anyone has had time to think about the first one.

| 57–61 | Miss G again supplies a brief answer and discussion only develops because Mr. S is prepared to admit that he does not understand. |
| 62–63 | What can one say to a remark like this? With just the right touch, Miss G gives no offence but adopts a faintly humorous approach. |

64　MRS. EVANS　I remember those verses. They're about the fruit of the Spirit being love, joy, peace and all those things, aren't they?

65　MRS. MONTGOMERY (pompously)　The fruit of the Spirit is love, joy, peace, patience, kindness, goodness, fidelity, gentleness and self control.

66　MRS. EVANS　Doesn't the NEB call it the harvest of the Spirit? That's a very helpful idea, I think, as if there is a whole lot of it, all waiting to burst out. I once spent some time doing private nursing on a farm at harvest time, and it was marvellous to see the harvest being reaped. It made me think about all the parts of the Bible where harvest is mentioned, and I looked them all up and had a lovely time reading them. My Bible means such a lot to me. I take it everywhere, you know, and it's surprising how often you just want to check up on something.

67　MRS. MONTGOMERY　Oh. I agree. Why, only last week on the bus I used mine when a lady sat next to me who needed to meet the Saviour. I showed her the verse in John . . .

68　MISS G　Thank you, Mrs. Montgomery. It might be better to get on with this passage just now, and we will hear about that interesting meeting a bit later on, when we are having coffee.
　　Is that part fairly clear about the fruit, Mr. S? Good. Mr. Montrose, what was your first question?

69　MR. MONTROSE　We were puzzled about the Father giving everything we ask.

70　MISS G　Oh, yes, in verse 16. That is a problem, isn't it? Perhaps the key to it lies in the phrase 'in My name'.

71　MRS. MONTGOMERY (piously)　Yes, that's right. If we ask for *spiritual* things, we shall get them.

72　MR. WARNER　It's not just spiritual things, though, is it? We can ask for all sorts in His name and provided it really is 'in His name', that is, in accordance with His will — we will get it.

73　MRS. BANKS　But how do we know it is His will? I never know what I ought to ask for.
　　The discussion continues for a further ten minutes.

74　MISS G　Can we move on now to the second column, please. I'm sorry we haven't dealt with all the points in the question section but time is passing. What action do you think we need to take, Mr. Peters?

75　MR. PETERS　The first we had was in verse 12 where it says we should love one another.

76　MISS G　Thank you. What did you note down, Mr. Warner?

77　MR. W　I felt that there were several implied points which were not explicitly stated. In verse 10, we can take the subordinate conditional clause 'If you heed My commandments' as an instruction.

64–68 Mrs. E and Mrs. M are in full flow, but are tactfully recalled. Miss G wisely ensures that the questioner is satisfied with the answers offered. One of the main points in raising the questions is lost if the questioner is left unsatisfied, if further help could have been given.

69–73 Miss G is once more the first to comment on the question but as she does not attempt to give an exhaustive answer, there is room for further comment and a useful discussion arises, based on Mrs. B's problem.

74 What should a leader do when the time is passing too quickly? Miss G opts to push the meeting along rather than to deal in any depth with the points which arise. It is always a wrench to move on from a section on which all your notes have not been utilized, but it is sometimes necessary to do so. Presumably in this group everyone had offered one of their prepared questions, so everyone would be at least partially satisfied.

75–76 Even at the risk of not covering all the points, comments such as Mr. Peters' should be discussed and applied. Clarity is being inadvisedly sacrificed to speed! It is difficult to avoid the Scylla and Charybdis of being beaten by the clock and being so succinct as to be unhelpful.

(Silence.)

78  MRS. SMITHSON  Whatever are talking about, please?

79  MISS G (briskly)  I know what he means, Mrs. Smithson. What other points for action did people have?

80  MRS. EVANS  I had verse 3, 'dwell in Me as I in you'. I think it is very important. In fact, it's really the centre of the Christian faith, isn't it? Once when I was . . .

81  MR. W (kindly)  I think Miss Griffiths has her eye on the clock, Mrs. Evans, and is trying to hurry us on a bit.

82  MRS. EVANS  I am sorry, dear. Yes, do carry on. I like to reminisce, and you must stop me.

83  MISS G  Thank you very much. It's very interesting, but we are a bit pushed for time. Any more points, please?

84  MRS. MONTGOMERY  In verse 7, He speaks about 'My words dwelling in you.' Now, that's important. It is definitely something we should take action on. How many of you read the Bible every day? I do. There's no point in trying to be a good, enthusiastic Christian if you don't read your Bible. It's what God intended us to do, or else He wouldn't have provided it.

85  MRS. SMITHSON  But how do you know what it means? We do try to read it, but even in this new Bible we sometimes can't make head or tail of it, can we, Frank?

86  MR. SMITHSON  You're right, dear. It sometimes leaves us feeling a bit puzzled. Perhaps we shouldn't have started with Romans.

87  MRS MONTGOMERY (dogmatically)  Oh, no, you should have started with John's gospel. That's the place to start.

88  MR. WARNER  There are several suitable places to start, aren't there? John's gospel is perhaps as good as any. Do you use any notes to help you, Mr. and Mrs. Smithson?

89  MR. S  Notes? What do you mean?

90  MRS. MONTGOMERY  He means Scripture Union notes. They give a passage for each day and a paragraph explaining it.

91  MR. W  Well, I didn't have those notes in mind, because I use the International Bible Reading Association ones, but there are various societies which produce them, and I'm sure they are all helpful.

92  MR. S  We will be very glad of anything which would be a help, thank you.

93  MRS. EVANS  I have some spare Bible Reading Fellowship notes and some Scripture Union notes, because I take them both, so I will let you have them next week. I find that now I have retired, I have time to do one in the morning and one in the evening, so I have two different kinds, to get the variety.

94  MISS G  Thank you. We will get back to the passage, shall we? We still have quite a lot of ground to cover . . .
The meeting proceeds.

77–79  The fact that Miss G understands is not enough! In her eagerness not to waste time, she has forgotten that the group is there to learn!

80–83  Everything is being sacrificed to brevity and speed! The members will be out of breath!

84–93  At last some general discussion is permitted. Perhaps Miss G has found she needs this time to catch her breath. Provided repetition and irrelevancies are cut to a minimum, discussion is important even if time is short.

Mr. W says what needs to be said and Mrs. E offers practical help.

Miss G is wise to leave them to it.

94  We can only hope that Miss G steers an even course throughout the remainder of the meeting, and that the study is completed in the time available without the group members feeling frustrated because too many subjects have been speedily opened and closed.

# HOUSE GROUP
## Details

Mr. and Mrs. Lambert moved into a particular corner of suburbia two years ago. They joined a local church, and there, and through the local council of churches, met various other couples who were interested in group Bible study. The present series of three meetings was planned to introduce non-Christian neighbours to the Christian faith.

The meetings have been held fortnightly, at the home of Mr. and Mrs. Lambert, and this is the final one of the present series.

## Members

| | |
|---|---|
| MR. ALAN LAMBERT | aged 34; Christian; lectures in Physics. |
| MRS. BETTY LAMBERT | aged 34; trained as secretary, now housewife. |
| MR. DONALD FRANKS | aged 35; in insurance; used to go to church, but moved and did not join in the new area; neighbours of Lamberts. |
| MRS. ANGELA FRANKS | aged 32; part-time nurse; little church interest. |
| MR. ERIC MONTROSE | aged 50; civil servant; regular churchgoer. |
| MRS. IRENE MONTROSE | similar outlook to Mr. M. |
| MISS PAMELA BROWN | aged 27; hospital pharmacist; Christian. |
| MR. BARRY ANDERSON | aged 42; teacher; mature Christian. |
| MRS. CAROL ANDERSON | aged 40; florist; mature Christian. |
| MR. LESLIE BROOMLEY | aged 30; never been to church; freelance photographer. |
| MRS. VERONICA BROOMLEY | aged 30; rarely been to church; writes children's stories; neighbours of the Lamberts. |
| MR. ERIC SMITHSON | aged 45; printing works manager; recently started attending church with their teenage children, who have become Christians recently. |
| MRS. BERYL SMITHSON | aged 44; housewife. |
| MR. PHILIP STANLEY | aged 40; lectures in biochemistry; has intellectual objections to Christianity. |

It is 7.50, and most of the members of the group have assembled in Mr. and Mrs. Lambert's sitting room where screen, projector and tape recorder are set up. There is an additional tape near the recorder, and on the door is fastened a large sheet of paper with the heading 'Who is Jesus Christ?' Nearby is a felt-tipped pen.

1     ALAN LAMBERT  It's good to see you all again. Mr. and Mrs. Montrose will be here soon after 8.0, as they have a parish communion for St. Andrew's day, but they have asked us to start without them.

    This is the third and final meeting of our present series based on the soundstrip 'Head in the Sand' and the subject for today is the third question raised by the strip, 'Who is Jesus Christ?' This is a vitally important question and one which we can profitably consider for a long time without exhausting the subject. As it is a few weeks since we saw the strip, we thought we would look at it again tonight to refresh our memories before we discuss the question, so here goes. Lights out, please, Betty.

(The lights go out and the soundstrip is shown. After ten minutes there is a commotion when Mr. and Mrs. Montrose arrive and find somewhere to sit. The soundstrip lasts 18 minutes. The lights are put on again and everyone waits.)

2     BETTY LAMBERT  It's surprising how much you miss the first time you see a filmstrip, isn't it? I've noticed several new points this time. Has anyone else?

3     DONALD FRANKS  Yes, it struck me how the end part, about racial problems and parent-teenager relationships and world hunger and so on, isn't just an appendix of moral teaching, bearing no relation to the rest of it, but it's an integral part of the Christian faith, isn't it? I mean, I don't know a great deal about it, but it just occurred to me that people who have worked out the answers to the three questions probably also have some sort of approach to these social aid moral issues. Do you think so?

4     BARRY ANDERSON  Yes, you've hit the nail on the head, Donald. When you've sorted out what is the point of life, and you realize it's God who runs the world, and have had a personal encounter with Jesus Christ and know Him as Saviour and Lord, then you get a new slant on social issues. And as the strip suggested, the Bible is where the teaching on all these things is to be found.

5     ERIC SMITHSON  It's funny you should say that, Donald, because our son and daughter have opened our eyes to a lot of things recently. They both went to young people's house-parties this summer and both came back claiming they had become Christians while they were there. We were a bit sceptical at first, because you know what kids are – all for this thing today, and by tomorrow they have completely lost interest in that, and are sold on something quite different. Anyway, Andrew and Pat have stuck to their guns for a few months now, and have got us going to church with them. In fact, it was they who got us coming here, through your kids, Barry and Carol. They told us they thought we ought to! Anyway, one thing I've particularly

# HOUSE GROUP
Sample 2

## METHOD
## 11 👁
AUDIO
VISUAL
AID

## METHOD
## 12 🐉
CHARACTER
STUDY

# HOUSE GROUP
## Details

A house meeting for Bible study at which any one is welcome, regardless of age, denomination or any other difference, can be very helpful. When a group of Christians has been established, a semi-evangelistic series such as this, to which interested neighbours are invited, can have far-reaching effects. It is a good way of preparing for a mission. In fact, several scattered house groups such as this could form the main outreach in a mission. Such meetings can also of course be an end in themselves, depending solely on the initiative of a small number of people who have a concern for their neighbours.

## Members

There is a good selection of Christian and non-Christian members here. It can be difficult to hold a Bible study with a large proportion of non-Christians present. On the other hand, an evangelistic Bible study is obviously out of place amongst a group composed entirely of committed Christians.

The Lamberts have prepared everything that will be needed for the meeting.

1   There is no delay and the meeting makes a crisp start. This gives a better impression than a half-hearted or staggered start. Even though some members are not expected until later, it is better to start promptly, otherwise the start tends to be later and later each meeting. On this occasion, the time before the latecomers arrived was utilized for reviewing the soundstrip, and not doing anything new.

2   A general comment with opportunity for other people to make observations is a useful beginning.

3–4   General comments such as these give the leaders a clue to the topics which interest the group members, and can reveal any misunderstandings they may have. It can also suggest a starting point for discussion.

67

noticed since they were converted, as they call it, is that they've both got involved in helping other people. Andrew calls at an old lady's house twice a week on his way home from school and does her shopping and odd jobs, and Pat goes every Saturday to help in the blind school. Just the other day I asked Pat about it, and she said that Jesus Christ had done so much for her that she wanted to do something for others of His children. It was a new idea to us, wasn't it, Beryl?

6    BERYL SMITHSON  It certainly was! And do you know, they actually get up on a Sunday morning to go to a Bible study before church? I had a job getting them out of bed before lunch time before!

7    BETTY LAMBERT  Yes, it does make a difference when people find the answer to this third question on the strip, 'Who is Jesus Christ?' We probably all have our own ideas on the subject, but before we air them we'll look at an incident in the New Testament to see how much we can learn about Jesus from there. After all, these are the records written by the people who knew Him when He was on earth, so that seems the best place to start.

We've got a set of New English Bibles here, so if you will all take one, please, and find John's gospel, chapter 4, we'll look at it. All got one? Good. We want to look at the first 42 verses except for a bit in the middle. It's the incident in which Jesus met a Samaritan woman — and it's important to remember that the Jews and the Samaritans were bitter enemies and would normally have nothing to do with each other. In spite of that, Jesus actually opened a conversation with this woman. For a man to talk casually to a woman was unusual in those days; for a Jewish man to talk to a Samaritan was unheard of, and for Him to talk to a woman of ill repute, as this woman was, was very much frowned upon. Let's see how much we can learn about the character of Jesus from the incident. We've got a tape recording here of the passage being read in the New English version by a narrator, Jesus, the Samaritan woman and, right at the end, Samaritan men. You'll probably recognize some of the voices, as the young people made the recording a couple of weeks ago when they were studying this passage. You'll be able to follow it in your Bibles. We miss out verses 31 to 38 by the way. (The tape is played while the group members follow in their Bibles.)

8    VERONICA BROOMLEY  I say, that's the devil of a good story. You know, it has an introduction, a central section with plenty of interest, and a satisfactory conclusion. I couldn't have written a better one myself! They read it awfully well, didn't they? I like that bit where Jesus has caught the woman out on this matter of her several 'husbands' and she quickly changes the subject to talk

5–6      This is an interesting contribution, though rather off the subject planned for the evening. The leaders now need to decide whether to pursue this line, or to introduce the planned subject.

7      Betty cleverly brings the subject round, without silencing the other members, but by relating what they have said to the subject in hand. It is a good idea to provide Bibles in the same version, especially for a group where there are several people who may not have their own Bible, or not a modern version.

Betty gives a simple introduction to the passage, and gives time for people to find it. A general summary of the contents given in advance helps people to concentrate while listening to the passage read.

The use of a tape in this situation is valuable, because it makes the story live, and is more memorable than a reading aloud by people who are not familiar with it.

about where people should worship, or something! I warm to the poor soul – she wasn't to know that this man she was talking to would know all about her. It must have floored her! They got the atmosphere over awfully well, didn't they?

9  LESLIE BROOMLEY  Trust you to look on it that way. I can see it will be appearing as a children's story before long, with your name as authoress! Though I must admit I found myself picturing it as it happened, and deciding which bits would make good photographs!

10  ALAN LAMBERT (laughing)  You two can't leave your work behind, can you? As Betty has said, we want to find out all we can about the character of Jesus, though in passing you might like to comment on the Samaritan woman as well! We'll suggest general points first, then, if necessary we will go through the passage again to tie up loose ends.

11  VERONICA BROOMLEY (quietly)  Loose is certainly the word for this story – or the woman!

12  ALAN LAMBERT  I'll write up our findings on this piece of paper as we mention them. Over to you!

13  BERYL SMITHSON  I'll tell you what struck me. Jesus seemed to have so much time to talk. So many people these days are too busy, and are always in a hurry to get on with something else, but He wasn't like that, was He?

14  PAMELA BROWN  Yes, I was thinking that. He must have been easy to talk to, mustn't He?

15  ANGELA FRANKS  And it says He was tired, and that was why He sat down by the well in the first place, so that makes it even more surprising that He bothered, doesn't it?

16  BETTY LAMBERT  I remember, the first time I read this passage, how surprised I was to find that Jesus did actually get tired. It's something I had never thought of before. He did have human physical weakness, like us.

17  DONALD FRANKS  He seems to have been thirsty as well.

18  ALAN LAMBERT  Unless He just asked for water to get talking to the woman.

19  VERONICA BROOMLEY (laughing)  Oho, so it was like that, was it?

20  ALAN LAMBERT (smiling)  No, I don't think so! Perhaps I put that badly. I meant that He knew He could help her but wanted to get her to admit her need of Him, so engaged her in conversation.

21  PAMELA BROWN  Well, you know, He may have asked her for a drink of water to put Himself in debt to her, because you always feel more kindly disposed towards people you've helped, and it was a way of making her feel needed and so prepared to listen.

22  ANGELA FRANKS  That's an interesting thought, Pamela. You know, I think you're right. I think I tend to feel a bit

| 8–9 | Not a helpful start. The leaders need to change the tone of the meeting, and this can be difficult without being rude. |
| 10 | A sympathetic sense of humour is a help in many situations, and here it smooths the way to the subject in hand. Alan is business-like in his leadership, but he also puts members at ease. He recommends a 'free for all' on the passage, but along specific lines. The alternative would have been to have gone through verse by verse at the outset, but that method can be rather dreary. |
| 11 | Another unhelpful comment. What does the leader do? |
| 12 | Alan chooses to ignore it, as it is not worth making an issue of. Charting the findings is useful for reference during the meeting and as a record afterwards. |
| 13 | The contributions that follow are helpful and the meeting proceeds as planned. |
| 19 | Veronica is still in flippant mood. |
| 20 | Alan's good humour comes to the fore again, and he apologizes for a remark which could be misconstrued. Politeness and graciousness are essential qualities in a leader – even if the attitude and remarks of members are disruptive. It is important for a leader not to be, or appear to be, shocked by anything that group members say, except under exceptional circumstances where the members can be expected to know better. Christians, especially those who have been brought up in a strict way, are easily shocked by the attitudes of those with no faith, or a new-found faith. Although moral laxity or anti-Biblical teaching can never be condoned, those in a more fortunate position should never appear to judge others – and evident shock at other people's views amounts to judging. |

resentful towards people whose help I need, but I somehow warm to those who need me. Jesus was a darn good psychologist!

23 BARRY ANDERSON It was very humble of Him, anyway, to ask help of a woman like this, wasn't it? Whatever deep motive He may have had, He had to throw superiority to the wind. Most of us would probably feel ourselves above asking help from someone our people despised — yet here is the King of Kings doing that very thing!

24 ERIC MONTROSE Even the woman was a bit impressed. Look at verse 9.

25 ALAN LAMBERT Yes, and Jesus makes capital out of her remark, by introducing the much deeper subject of the living water.

Ten minutes later. The chart is filled in as follows.

Who is Jesus Christ?

(based on John 4)
Time for people
Easy to talk to
Became tired ⎫
Became thirsty ⎬ NB Human
Humble
Willing to be personally indebted
Good psychologist
Able to lead conversation naturally to vital subjects
Claims to be the Messiah — the Christ
Offers eternal life
Makes His offer attractive
Knows all about people
Held the respect of His disciples (27)
Caused people (e.g. Samaritan woman) to abandon what they were doing (water jar)
Attracted people (30)
Saviour of the world

26 ALAN LAMBERT These are our findings so far. Let's just glance back over the passage and see if we've missed anything, then we can look at the chart and see what general picture we get of Jesus.

(Pause while all read.)

A few other points emerge and are added to the list.

27 PHILIP STANLEY This list is all very impressive, but we must remember that the account we are studying was written by someone who had a vested interest in painting a glowing picture of Jesus.

28 DONALD FRANKS What do you mean? I'm a bit clueless about all this. Can you explain a bit more, please?

29 PHILIP STANLEY Well, doesn't John say somewhere, near the end of the gospel, I seem to remember, that he had written it all so that people would believe? So naturally he would depict Jesus in the best light possible. If, for

26       Constant reference to the passage is vital if the study is to be of maximum benefit.

27–37    A member who suddenly raises an intellectual problem of this kind can easily disturb the inexperienced leader. There is the danger of unceremoniously thrusting the issue to one side through a feeling of inability to deal with it; equally, there is the danger of giving a speedy and glib answer in an attempt to silence the enquiry.

Alan is fully prepared to have the subject discussed, which in this situation is the wisest approach as it can be damaging for a person with real intellectual difficulties to have them ignored.

In 31 Alan deals very pleasantly with Veronica's somewhat rambling remarks and does not respond to her final provocative question (in 30) with a forceful evangelistic message, which a less mature leader could have been tempted to do.

instance, one of the Pharisees had taken it upon himself to write an account of the life of Jesus, the effect on us would have been vastly different. I don't think we can with intellectual honesty accept this gospel of John's or any of the others, for that matter, as a totally unbiased report of what happened – that is, if it happened at all!

30   VERONICA BROOMLEY  It's very interesting to hear you say that, Philip. I tend to agree with your point of view, but somehow while we were reading this passage through tonight, I forgot that it's just a story – and the devil of a good one, at that! It seemed to make Jesus a real person, with flesh and blood and personality. It's just because it *is* so well written, of course, that we are kind of brain-washed into accepting it as true. It's like some of the good novels you can read – you finish up really believing in the existence of the characters. Good grief! If I could write children's stories like that! I'd be worth a packet in next to no time. Though as I come to think of it, you very religious types would probably have some highly spiritualized reason for the effect this particular story has on me! Am I about to be converted, do you think? (she emits a high-pitched laugh).

31   ALAN LAMBERT (lightly)  We're not in the best position to say about that, Veronica! That's something between you and God. But you are right in thinking that we would give a different reason for the fact that in spite of yourself, you find this story convincing – and that's simply that it's true! But let's go back to Philip's point: would you like to comment on it, Barry?

32   BARRY ANDERSON  You mean the point that the gospel writers didn't tell the whole truth?

33   ALAN LAMBERT  Yes, please. Philip and I have been over the same ground here several times, and it might be a good idea to get a different slant on it.

34   BARRY ANDERSON  H'm. I'm not too sure I can put it into adequate words, but I'll burble on for a minute and we'll see where we get to. As a matter of fact, I think there may be something in this idea that the gospel writers told only what they wanted us to know. After all, who wouldn't? But my view is that the life of Jesus was perfect in every way, so that even an unbiased account would inevitably present Him as a good chap. The accusers at His trial had to concoct accusations, didn't they, and Pilate couldn't find anything wrong with Him. So although I would be inclined to agree that the gospel writers missed out many details, they wouldn't be deliberately falsifying the picture – because they didn't need to! Jesus' goodness was there for all to see, and they selected the facts which would help readers to see the truth.

    So that's what I think! Is that the sort of thing you had in mind, Alan, or am I barking up the wrong tree?

31–34 It is helpful for the leader to draw in other members of the group to comment on points raised, as it avoids the awkward situation of the leader and one other member engaging in a prolonged dialogue to the exclusion of other members.

In 35 and 37 Alan adopts the light touch and does not try to press for decisions or agreement. It is often better to have the Christian case stated and to leave it there, rather than to pursue the point to the end, unless the questioning member himself indicates that he wants to take it further.

Reference back to the soundstrip helps to make the meeting an entirety rather than disjointed parts. Here it serves to highlight the contrast between the Biblical findings and the general view of the world.

Once the list has been compiled, it is helpful to stand back, as it were, and take a long view of it. The comments which follow touch upon basic issues of the Christian faith, and all arise directly from the group's corporate findings. These questions (in 50, 53 and 55) are unlikely to have arisen in general discussion, but occur naturally in this context.

35　ALAN LAMBERT (smiling)　That's just the sort of thing, thanks, Barry. Convinced, Philip?

36　PHILIP　Not yet! I'll take more convincing than that, that Christianity is intellectually acceptable! There are several points which need explaining before I shall be on your side of the fence! There's the small matter of the virgin birth, and the unlikely story of the resurrection, and that little matter of the semi-literate disciples suddenly having the ability to speak in different languages! Oh, no, you don't convince me in one fell swoop! Though I am prepared to listen and I certainly admire your sincerity.

37　ALAN LAMBERT　There's hope for you yet, Philip!
　　　Well, we seem to have compiled a nice jumble of answers to the question 'Who is Jesus?' You may remember some of the answers the filmstrip suggested.
　　　'Is Christ just a reason for celebrating Christmas? Did He merely give His name to a commercial racket?
　　　Who was He really? The founder of the "League against Everything"?
　　　Was He simply a great teacher to be put alongside Confucius and Plato, Buddha and Karl Marx?
　　　Was He merely a sentimental figure to be caricatured in stained glass and slushy sentimental hymns?
　　　Was He a political Deliverer, as many people thought?'
　　　The points we have made seem rather different, don't they? Are there any general comments on our findings?

38　DONALD FRANKS　It's a real eye-opener to me, looking at this passage. I didn't realize there was so much to this man, Jesus Christ. I must confess that I have always thought of Him as a stained-glass window sort of figure. But He's so human, isn't He?

39　CAROL ANDERSON　And yet He is divine as well. That's the marvellous thing, isn't it? He was — or is — the Christ, the expected Messiah, who brought this living water to mankind.

40　PHILIP STANLEY　That's another thing, while I'm in the mood to raise objections. You claim that Jesus was both human and divine. Was He half and half? And if so, which bits were which?

41　VERONICA BROOMLEY　Good Lord, that's a thought! If he were my man, I know which parts I would want to be human!

42　LESLIE BROOMLEY　Steady on, Ronnie, that's going a bit far.

43　VERONICA BROOMLEY　Oh, sorry I spoke. Just thought things were getting a bit too serious.

44　PHILIP STANLEY　Well, yes, I *am* serious. Biologically, it seems to me to be an unlikely phenomenon.

45　ALAN　It *is* unlikely, but you would be the first to admit, Philip, that in science it is often the unlikely things that

40 A huge question which anyone but a theologian would hesitate to tackle. How will Alan respond?

41–43 A brief respite for Alan, who wisely ignores these unhelpful remarks.

turn out to be true. But this particular matter isn't a bio-logical truth. His body was human. The complexity comes in His nature — the very essence of Himself, and that was both fully human and fully divine. Mind you, I don't claim to begin to understand it but in my clearer moments I can dimly realize the truth of it. It's one of those Biblical paradoxes that we have to take on trust for now. But it will be tremendous when we see Him in all His glory, and understand all these things!

46   LESLIE BROOMLEY  You mean to say you actually believe in heaven, and all that nonsense? I didn't think any intelligent people believed any of that! You *do* surprise me!

47   ALAN LAMBERT  Yes, I certainly do believe in heaven, Leslie.

48   ANGELA FRANKS  In my nursing I meet loads of people who don't believe in heaven until they are faced with death, and suddenly they start praying, and all kinds of things! I've always found it a bit sickening. It's like taking out an insurance policy when your house is on fire — a useless measure, and a bit cowardly somehow.

49   BETTY LAMBERT  Yes, it is sad when people only realize their need of God when things go wrong in their lives. It's much wiser to think things out when you can do it rationally without any crisis colouring the picture. When you come to a firm, deep faith in God through Jesus Christ, these traumatic experiences, like facing death, can be taken much more in one's stride, and in full trust in God. However, have we any more comments on the chart as it stands at the moment?

50   LESLIE BROOMLEY  I don't get this living water idea. Sounds a bit odd to me. Can someone explain it?

51   BARRY ANDERSON  In this passage it's tied up with eternal life, in verse 14, and Jesus being the Messiah, in verse 25, and the Saviour of the world in verse 42. He came to earth to make a link between God and man — the link that had been broken by man's sin — and so to give the opportunity of eternal life.

52   IRENE MONTROSE  And the Samaritan woman was cert-ainly a sinner! Jesus soon put his finger on that, didn't He?

53   BERYL SMITHSON (thoughtfully)  But you know, Andrew and Pat were saying the other day that we are all sinners — not only people like this woman, and folk who are obvious sinners. It seemed a funny idea to me, but I wonder if they had something.

54   BETTY LAMBERT  Yes, we get to feel a bit complacent because we are better than some people, don't we? But even though we might not be too bad by the world's standards, we are sinners by God's standards. And we all need a Saviour because of that. That's why Jesus is the Saviour of the world.

| 45 | How wise to admit ignorance in a case like this! A leader's admission that he doesn't know, coupled with a brief explanation of how he views the problem, is far more helpful than dogmatic statements thought up on the spur of the moment. |
| 46–47 | Scornful disbelief is met with quiet confidence which gives a better impression than a heated response would have done. |
| 49 | Arising out of the last comment, Betty quotes her own personal experience and then gently leads the group back to the chart. |

It is difficult to know just when to return to the original point, and a leader needs to be sensitive to the reactions of the group in order to select the right moment to do it. Important subjects raised should be aired, but should not normally be allowed to dominate the meeting if the consideration of other points would help to give a balanced picture of the main subject under review.

55 BERYL SMITHSON  You say 'is' the Saviour of the world, and I notice the soundstrip said 'Who *is* Jesus Christ?' You mean He is alive today?

(The discussion continues for a further ten minutes after which the meeting is closed with a prayer by Betty Lambert. While coffee is being served, the subject of the next meeting is raised.)

56 PAMELA BROWN  What are we doing next time?

57 ERIC SMITHSON  Yes, what are we doing? I've been thinking about it, and I'd be grateful if we could discuss strikes, because it's a thing that's threatening at our printing works. Flaming nuisance it is, too. I thought you people might have some ideas on it.

58 ANGELA FRANKS  And then can we discuss depression some time? I meet so many people in the hospital who are depressed, and it's not just the patients. One of the nursing staff has had to go into a psychiatric hospital this last week with acute depression and I often feel a bit that way myself. Is there a Christian answer to it? You people, who seem to have a real faith, as opposed to those of us who just do or don't go to church, might be able to give a lead on this.

59 BETTY LAMBERT  We certainly haven't any slick answers to either of those problems, but we could probably deal with them somehow, couldn't we, Alan?

60 ALAN LAMBERT  Yes, though I don't think just discussing them will help a lot, and the Bible doesn't really give direct advice about strike action. However, we could perhaps study a passage about community life, and relationships, and some of it would give us some indication about what attitude to adopt in a strike situation.

61 BARRY ANDERSON  There's that bit in Ephesians about husbands and wives, and parents and children, and slaves and masters, isn't there? That might help.

62 CAROL ANDERSON  Yes, it's in chapters 5 and 6, isn't it? Then there's a similar bit in Colossians 3.

63 ALAN LAMBERT  I'll see about preparing a study on various passages for next time then, shall I? Then what about Angela's depression — sorry, Angela, I mean your topic, not your depression!

64 PAMELA BROWN  There's a Christian psychiatrist at the hospital where I work, and he might come and give us a talk about it.

65 BETTY LAMBERT  That's a good idea, Pamela, and then we could have a Bible study on the fruit of the Spirit — you know, love, joy, peace and so on, or on John 15, the true vine. That might be helpful.

66 ALAN LAMBERT  Good. Will you contact your psychiatrist man, then, Pamela, and get him whenever he can come, and we'll plan it from there.

The members ultimately disperse.

Between 55 and 56  Should a meeting always be opened and closed in prayer? There was no opening prayer on this occasion. Was this an omission? Or is the closing prayer an intrusion? The answer depends very much on the type of meeting, and the group members. Simply because there is no audible prayer, all prayer is not automatically excluded, and much prayer should have gone into the preparation of any Bible study. If prayer would embarrass group members, it should usually be avoided, although it may often be found, as here, that it seems natural at the end, though artificial at the beginning. Leaders should consider carefully what is appropriate in each situation, and not assume that one way is always right. When a group of Christians meet they will naturally want to ask for God's guidance.

57–58  Requests for Bible study on given subjects are often made, and can constitute a problem where the subject is not mentioned specifically in the Bible. Even where there are occasional references to the subject throughout the Bible, a study based on out-of-context texts is unlikely to be profitable. However, such subjects should not be shelved permanently, and some solution must be found.

60  Alan has one solution – to look at a more general subject which embraces the specific topic requested, and on which there is clear Biblical teaching. Principles can be drawn from this and applied to more specific problems.

64  On a difficult topic such as depression, it is helpful to have the benefit of the knowledge and experience of an expert. Much harm can be done by enthusiastic but ill-advised Christians picking out verses to support their own ideas.

65  Betty adopts the same principle as Alan, and suggests a study of a general and positive nature which will give some guidance on the matter in hand. The 'Christian answer' to such problems will only emerge from a deep study of the Bible over a period of time, and cannot be produced like a rabbit out of a hat, on demand.

# YOUNG WIVES' GROUP
## Details

A fortnightly meeting on church premises, and technically a church activity, although only a few of the members attend church regularly.

## Members

MRS. LAMBERT  (see House Group sample)
MRS. FREDERICKS  *aged 35, used to go to church.*
MRS. NORMANTON  *aged 38; sympathetic to church activities.*
MRS. TEDDING  *has three children, aged 5, 7 and 10; ambitious.*
MRS. HARRISON  *actively engaged in church bazaars, bring and buy sales, etc.*
MRS. SANDERSON  *minister's wife; eager to please all.*
MRS. MONTGOMERY  *aged 25; over-zealous, Christian, rather tactless.*
MRS. BARCLAY  *aged 32; has three boys; quiet.*
MRS. PLUMMER  *has two children under 5; first meeting.*

## Text

It is 7.20 and Mrs. Lambert, Mrs. Sanderson and Mrs. Montgomery are at the church early to prepare the room, and the teacups. Other members gradually assemble and discuss the last meeting — a corset demonstration.

1  MRS. SANDERSON  That was a first-rate corset demonstration last time, wasn't it? My husband laughed when he heard what we were doing, but I thought it was very good, and I am thinking about ordering some from her.

2  MRS. LAMBERT  Yes, it was interesting. You weren't here, were you, Mrs. Montgomery?

3  MRS. MONTGOMERY  No, I only attend the *spiritual* meetings. I think it is quite wrong to have non-religious meetings on church premises.

4  MRS. HARRISON (just arriving)  What was that? Surely everything that happens here is religious. My children were just saying as I came out that I am the most religious person they know, because I'm always at church.

5  MRS. M  I don't agree — there are religious and non-religious meetings held here, and as I said, *I* only attend the religious ones.

6  MRS. S (soothingly)  Oh, come now, Mrs. Montgomery, surely you don't think there shouldn't be any other meetings? We can't be holy all the time, can we? It's much better to have a nice, balanced programme, with demonstrations and visits to the shows, and speakers and Bible studies.

82

# YOUNG WIVES' GROUP

Sample 3

## METHOD

# 10

TOPICAL
STUDY

## METHOD

# 12

CHARACTER
STUDY

## Members

An interesting group in which only a few hold firm Christian beliefs, but in which several are sympathetic. It is a small, recently-formed group with no specific leader, because Mrs. Sanderson, the minister's wife, who initiated it, was not prepared to lead it. Each member in turn takes responsibility for a meeting.

1      In a group such as this, where there is a wide range of activities, a Bible study is unlikely to be very popular, although if presented with enthusiasm and imagination it can be effective. The situation is a challenge, and the meeting needs careful planning and skilful leadership if it is to be successful.

3–5    A particularly pious member can be more of a hindrance than a help in a group of this kind. We shall need to watch Mrs. M! Mrs. Harrison's approach is hardly more helpful. Whoever is to lead has a difficult assignment, as a bad atmosphere is already developing and will be difficult to eradicate.

6      A peacemaker! Mrs. Sanderson tries to promote harmony, but is in danger of being indecisive as a result.

7     MRS. M   No, I think the other activities are most unsuitable for Christians, and I only come at all because I think some-one might be won for Christ by my words and witness.

8     MRS. H (bossily)   Is everyone here? It's time we were starting.

      (Enter Mrs. Barclay and Mrs. Plummer.)

9     MRS. BARCLAY   This is Mrs. Plummer, my neighbour, who said she would like to join us. She doesn't get out much, as she has two youngsters.

10    MRS. H   Oh, hello. We were just about to start. Who is taking this meeting?

11    MRS. L   It was supposed to be Mrs. Tedding, but she isn't here yet, and then Mrs. Montgomery is leading the Bible study part.

12    MRS. H   Dear, dear, I do like meetings to start promptly. It's too bad of her to be late.

13    MRS. S   I expect something cropped up at the last minute. Shall we have a hymn and a prayer and she might be here by then?

      (They hurriedly choose and sing a hymn, with Mrs. S. at the badly tuned piano. Mrs. L agrees to open in prayer, during which Mrs. Tedding rushes in.)

14    MRS. TEDDING   So sorry I'm late, ladies. I see you have started. Before we do our Bible study which someone else is going to lead – who is it? Mrs. Montgomery, yes, I remember now. Well, as I was saying, before that, I want to tell you a story, and we can discuss a problem it raises. Now, where did I put my notes? Ah, yes, here they are.

      Mr. and Mrs. Patterson were an ordinary, good-living couple, with no children, several friends, and an average income. One day, quite out of the blue, they had a tele-phone call from a solicitor to say that Mr. Patterson's uncle had died, and that they were beneficiaries in his will. When they visited the solicitor next day and heard the contents of the will, they were amazed to find out that the uncle had left them £10,000. However, there was one condition attached, and that was that £1,000 was to be given intact to some charity or good cause.

      At first they thought nothing of this, and were naturally delighted with the windfall. When they came to decide who should have the £1,000, they couldn't agree. Mrs. Patterson wanted to give it to the church she attended, which had just launched an appeal for a much-needed extension to the premises, but Mr. Patterson, who was very fond of children, wanted it to go to the Save the Children Fund, which he had always supported generously. They could not split the £1,000, as the uncle's will had said it was to be given intact to one good cause, otherwise they would forfeit the remaining £9,000.

      Well, there it is. It's an odd sort of story, but there are

| 7 | Mrs. M is bent on establishing her point, even if this is detrimental to the atmosphere. |
|---|---|
| 8 | Here we meet an 'organizer'. People like this can be found in most groups, and there is very little we can do about them, except to ensure that they are not us! Organizing ability can be channelled in useful directions, and the organizer can be prevented from interfering in other people's concerns. |
| 9 | The timing of the introduction of a new member needs to be planned carefully. Mrs. Barclay presumably felt that a Bible study was a better introduction for Mrs. Plummer than a corset demonstration. (It is sometimes worth inviting a friend to a particular meeting a few weeks hence, rather than issuing a general invitation for any time.) |
| 10 | Whatever the meeting, a warmer welcome than this should be offered, although a gushing one can be equally unacceptable. |
| 11 | Hardly a promising beginning — and whatever will be the group's response to Mrs. M's leadership?! |
| 12–13 | The best-laid plans can go wrong, and the situation is speedily remedied by two capable ladies. |
| 14 | Whatever the cause of the delay, Mrs. Tedding will feel inadequately prepared because of the rush. If possible (and it must be said that it is not always possible, because of family demands), people taking part in a meeting should be present early in order to prepare themselves and their equipment. |

It appears that the two people who are taking part in this meeting have not got together to plan and pray. Particularly where the two parts of the meeting are closely linked, co-ordination is essential, and it is always helpful to spend time with a co-leader.

Mrs. Tedding does not give a satisfactory introduction to the method being adopted, and gives the impression that there are two separate parts to the meeting. She could have mentioned that her story poses a problem to which the subsequent Bible study will offer a solution.

She tells the story simply and well, without unnecessary detail, but with sufficient background information to give a clear idea of the situation and the problem.

some eccentric people about, and it seems it really happened. I read it in a magazine. The question is, what should they do with the money?

15   MRS. FREDERICKS   I would say it was quite obvious. It should go to the Save the Children Fund, because that would do far more good than building extra rooms for the church, which is badly attended anyway, most likely.

16   MRS. M   But if extending the church premises meant that more people would hear the gospel, that would be best.

17   Mrs. H   Well, apart from all the religious stuff that goes on in a church, it does plenty of good in many ways. Look at the way the last Bring and Buy sale produced money for the National Children's Home. The money would help the church *and* the children, if it went to our church extension fund!

    The discussion continues in similar vein.

18   MRS. T   We've aired our views on that now. Mrs. Montgomery is going to lead us in a Bible study, to see if a Biblical incident will give us any clues to the principles involved in a situation like this.

19   MRS. M   Yes, we will first of all pray that God will help us to understand His holy word and that He will speak to each one of us with some message that goes right to our hearts and shows us what sinners we are – all of us – and how much we need Him, and how He can help us to live as He would have us live.

    (Mrs. M. prays at great length along these lines.)

20   MRS. M   This is the important part of the evening, so open your Bibles at John 12. Everyone got it? Oh, I see, you haven't got Bibles. That's a bit of a problem.

21   MRS. S   There are some in the minister's vestry. Shall I go and get them?

22   MRS. M   Yes, please. What a pity you didn't all bring one with you. I always carry mine wherever I go – you never know when you might meet some poor soul who is thirsty for the gospel.

    (Mrs. S eventually returns with an armful of Bibles, in varying translations.)

23   MRS. M   Thank you. Turn to John 12. 1 to 8. Mrs. Normanton, will you read verses 1 to 3 and Mrs. Plummer 4 to 8. You haven't found John? Well, everyone knows it is the fourth gospel – no, in the New Testament, you're looking in Psalms. You really ought to know your Bible better than that!

24   MRS. N (confused)   Oh, I'm sorry, I wasn't thinking. What was it you wanted me to read?

25   MRS. M   Verses 1 to 3, please, then, Mrs. – what was your name? – yes, Plummer to verse 8 please.

26   MRS. PLUMMER (hesitantly)   I would rather not, if you don't mind.

| 15–17 | The discussion on the problem goes well, and needs little steering. |
| 18 | At last Mrs. T explains how the story and the Bible study are connected — a point which people could be forgiven for not having grasped until now. |
| 19 | Mrs. M gives the impression that only now are they about to embark on the important part of the meeting, and she tends to discount the earlier part, without which her Bible study would be less meaningful. Her detailed account of what is to be prayed for is a mini-sermon, and one can safely assume that the prayer itself would be aimed at the members. |

Leaders should resist the temptation to pray at people in this way.

A prayer at this point in the meeting is not entirely appropriate, even if suitable sentiments are expressed.

| 20 | The abrupt introduction to the passage is cut short by the sad absence of the vital tool. Bad planning, Mrs. M ! |
| 21 | Rescued ! |
| 22 | Remarks of this kind are rarely, if ever, appropriate, and in a meeting such as this, most unwise. |
| 23 | A critical attitude does not help. If people are not familiar with the Bible, a rebuke is unlikely to evoke interest. |

| 27 | MRS. M | Nonsense! It will make you feel you belong. |
| 28 | MRS. P | I'm sorry, but it would be better if someone else did. |
| 29 | MRS. M | I'm sure you can do it very well. |
| 30 | MRS. P | I haven't brought my reading glasses, so I can't see too well. |
| 31 | MRS. M | Well, why didn't you say? Mrs. Barclay, will you read it please? |

(The passage is read, though with some difficulty as Mrs. N has an Authorized Version and Mrs. B a New English Bible.)

| 32 | MRS. M | Thank you. Now, let's do a little exercise in character study. Mrs. Normanton, Mrs. Fredericks and Mrs. Lambert, you study Mary. Mrs. Tedding, Mrs. Harrison and Mrs. Sanderson, study Jesus, and the rest study Judas. Then there is a Christian in each group. |
| 33 | MRS. S | (hesitantly) I don't think we are quite clear what you want us to do, Mrs. Montgomery. |
| 34 | MRS. M | Are you not? I want you to do a character study on each of these people. |
| 35 | MRS. L | You mean to find out as much as we can about each one, from this passage? |
| 36 | MRS. M | Yes, that's the idea. |
| 37 | MRS. B | Do you want us to write down what we find? |
| 38 | MRS. M | That's a good idea. Has anyone any paper? |
| 39 | MRS. S | I saw some scrap paper in the minister's vestry. Shall I get it? |
| 40 | MRS. M | Yes, if you will. |

(Pause until Mrs. S returns.)

| 41 | MRS. M | Each group can have one sheet. Has anyone anything to write with? No, oh dear! |
| 42 | MRS. S | I might be able to find something (exit). |
| 43 | MRS. H | (bustling) If you move your chair round here, Mrs. Tedding, and yours that way, Mrs. Fredericks, we can be in nice little circles. Good. Now we will be able to manage. |
| 44 | MRS. T | But I'm still not quite sure what you want us to do. |
| 45 | MRS. M | (with studied patience) Your group is studying Mary, Mrs. Fredericks, and you will be writing down all you can about her from this passage. |
| 46 | MRS. F | But doesn't that just mean copying bits out? |
| 47 | MRS. M | (rapidly losing patience) Of course not. You need to work out what you can about her from what she said and did. |
| 48 | MRS. S | You mean that we can work out that Judas was a hypocrite, and things like that? |
| 49 | MRS. M | Yes, that's right. Now, does everyone understand? |
| 50 | MRS. L | I think we are all fairly clear now, thank you. We will write down all we can learn about each character, and then put all our findings together to get the different slants |

| 24–31 | Mrs. M's schoolma'am approach does nothing to promote a relaxed atmosphere, and she is merciless in her insistence that the newcomer should participate. Most people making a first visit to a meeting would be grateful to observe at first, and to participate actively only after they have settled in. Mrs. M knows nothing about Mrs. Plummer, and it is unfair to ask her to do anything until she has given some indication of her abilities. Sight reading can be a formidable assignment to those unused to the sound of their own voices. |
|---|---|
| 32 | Mrs. M has given some thought to the division into groups, and has worked to a system. This is good, though she would have done better not to have pointed out her system to the group! She may feel it is best to have the Christians dispersed throughout the groups, but it is highly inadvisable to differentiate between those who are Christians and those who are not. |
| 33–36 | The instructions were inadequate. Mrs. M understands what she wants done, but it needs spelling out to those to whom it is a new idea. A more detailed account of what she had in mind would have avoided a lengthy discussion on the mechanics of the method. |
| 38–42 | How would Mrs. M manage without Mrs. S?! |
| 43–55 | Mrs. L quietly clarifies what is required, and Mrs. M finally loses patience. Whatever the problem, leaders should not lose patience. |

on the incident. We could write our findings on that blackboard over there, if we had some chalk, couldn't we? Then we would be able to see it all.

51 MRS. S (in a tired voice) I'll go and see if there is any chalk then.

52 MRS. T And how long did you say we had to make this list?

53 MRS. M I didn't say. Have as long as you need.

54 MRS. L Five minutes should be long enough, do you think?

55 MRS. M That should be sufficient. My goodness, you ladies do take some organizing!

(There follows five minutes of discussion in the groups, during which Mrs. S returns with a tiny piece of chalk, and Mrs. M sits reading her Bible on her own.)

56 MRS. M You have had your time, ladies!

57 MRS. N Oh, we have only just started. We got a bit off the subject at first.

58 MRS. M That's too bad of you!

59 MRS. N It was very important. We were finding out how often we each invited people for dinner.

60 MRS. M That has nothing at all to do with the subject! Oh, really!

61 MRS. NORMANTON It has — this story is about Jesus going out visiting, isn't it?

62 MRS. M Well, yes it is, but that's not the point of the story. We need to get on to the subject of the death of Jesus, and it's tremendous significance for all of us today, and how He can help us in all we do, and we should not be wasting time on trivialities!

63 MRS. S Would you like me to write on the board what we found out about Jesus?

64 MRS. M (mollified) Yes, please.

(This is done, without comment.)

65 MRS. B Shall I write up ours about Judas?

(This is done without comment.)

66 MRS. M We will all have to work out the points about Mary, as that group did not do it. Who will start?

(Ideas are put forward, and the chart finally looks like this.)

*Jesus*
Allows Mary to anoint Him
Sympathetic to genuine love
Rebukes hypocrite
Sees through Judas' false concern for others

| *Judas* | *Mary* |
| --- | --- |
| Outspoken | Did not serve at table |
| Hypocrite | Impetuous? |
| Thief | Generous |
| Tries to get Mary into trouble | Sees importance of Jesus |

| | |
|---|---|
| 56–61 | If Mrs. M had attended to the groups during the allotted five minutes, she might have been able tactfully to steer them on to the right lines. Her irritation is evident, and does not encourage co-operation. |
| 62 | Another mini-sermon, and irrelevant to the main subject under consideration. They appear to have lost track of this! |
| 63 | Mrs. S's timely intervention prevents a retort. |
| 64–65 | It is helpful if either the contributor or the leader gives a commentary as the findings are written up. This removes any doubt about the meaning of the brief notes, explains their source and makes the point more memorable. |
| 66 | Mrs. M is still annoyed about the time spent in the small group on 'trivialities' and makes this obvious. It is hard, when you have spent a long time working out a method, to have it ignored, and to see the time wasted. However, it is now too late for Mrs. M to do anything about it, and a more gracious spirit would help to create a better atmosphere. |

67 MRS. M That's done, then. The important thing is that Jesus was about to die – for our sin, for yours and mine, because we are all sinners. Do you realize that you are sinners? You were born in sin, and live in sin.

68 MRS. P Well! I'm not staying here to be insulted! First you try to make me read aloud, and then you insult me! I'm going! (storms out). There is a stunned silence.

69 MRS. S That was perhaps not put the best way, Mrs. Montgomery. She doesn't understand what you mean by sin.

70 MRS. B I'll go after her and try to explain, but I don't think she will come again. (Exit.)

71 MRS. L The point we had planned to consider was whether Mary should have used the expensive perfume on Jesus, or whether she should have sold it to give the money to the poor.

72 MRS. S Yes, that's the vital thing, isn't it? That's what your story was about, Mrs. Tedding.

73 MRS. F Oh, I see. I wondered what this had to do with that. Ah, well, it seems pretty clear that Jesus thought it right that the perfume should be used on Him, doesn't it? So do we assume that the lady and gentleman in your story should give the money to the church?

74 MRS. H But it's not as simple as that, is it? This was perhaps a special occasion to be lavished on Him, in preparation for His burial.

75 MRS. F Perhaps that church in the story felt that its appeal was special, too.

76 MRS. S Perhaps as the lady and gentleman – Patterson, wasn't it? – hadn't any family, they should have been prepared to forfeit the £9,000 and split the £1,000 between the two causes.

77 MRS. T Good Lord! No one in their right mind would do that!

78 MRS. M But you are not a Christian, Mrs. Tedding, so you wouldn't know about spiritual values.

79 MRS. T Well, really! Who do you think you are, the judge of the world?

80 MRS. S (mildly) You ought not to say things like that, Mrs. Montgomery. How can any of us know who is a Christian and who isn't, and who are we to judge?

81 MRS. M I can tell. Some people are spiritually-minded, and others are not.

82 MRS. L (firmly) That's not what we are discussing though, is it? We are trying to see if there are any principles we can learn from this passage which we could apply to everyday life, such as this incident we have outlined.

The meeting continues.

67      A direct evangelistic assault, and crucial, though the death of Jesus Christ is to the Christian faith, it is not the main point under consideration in this instance. Her abrupt denunciation of other members is uncalled for here, and her manner is unlikely to attract others to her Saviour. Even though her statements are true, they are likely to be misconstrued and therefore, rather than do any good, they will do harm.

68      An understandable reaction.

69–70  Even the most tolerant members are losing patience, but each is trying to smooth over a difficult situation. With a leader like Mrs. M, a supporting team of tactful members is vital. The new member will have made her last visit.

71–73  At last the point is made! It is not surprising that Mrs. F and probably others, felt confused! The major point under consideration needs reiterating several times in order to keep it at the forefront of members' minds.

73–76  This point should have been reached much sooner. The basis of the method adopted is to consider a problem, study a Biblical passage relating to that problem, and, in the light of any Biblical principles which emerge, reconsider the problem. This group has been badly led, and most of the members do not know what is expected of them. As the majority are unused to Bible study they need careful leadership, and gentle handling.

78      There she goes again! Her motives are doubtless admirable, but her methods disastrous!

82      To the rescue again!

It is possible, though unlikely, that the meeting will proceed satisfactorily.

The qualities of leadership which are most conspicuous by their absence in Mrs. M are patience and consideration for other people's feelings. Her zeal has made her insensitive to others and she has probably succeeded in finally killing the idea of Bible study, in this group.

# CHURCH FELLOWSHIP
## Details
Monthly meeting. Well-established. Cosy group — all know each other.

## Members

| | |
|---|---|
| MRS. MARSTON | *widow, late fifties; clear thinker; active in good works.* |
| MR. PETERS | *elderly, retired; rather negative; suspicious of youth.* |
| MRS. PETERS | *sweet and kind and shockable; sees good in everything.* |
| MISS CRAWFORD | *middle-aged; S.S. teacher; civil servant.* |
| MR. WATERS | *early forties; quantity surveyor, lay reader.* |
| MISS GRIFFITHS | *mid-twenties; teacher; well versed in Biblical matters.* |
| PAUL | *last year at school, about to go to University.* |
| PENNY AND SUSAN | *16 year old schoolgirls; inexperienced in Bible study* |
| REV. JOHN TILNEY | *visits occasionally; likes to have a Bible study group in his church.* |

## Method
Key questions. This is a variation on the Question and Answer method, which is the most common one for group Bible study, and can be effective in a group of comparatively mature Christians who are keen to study the Bible. If the questions are well-chosen and well-timed, the leader can be unobtrusive, merely steering the discussion in helpful directions, and coming to the rescue when it is in danger of getting out of hand. The method looks deceptively easy, but involves a great deal of preparation on the part of the leader. The use of the slips of paper containing questions to be discussed initially in pairs is a variation of the basic method.

## Content
This is the third in a series on the Sermon on the Mount. The passage for study is Matthew chapter 5, verses 10 and following. The leadership passes round and Mrs. Marston has prepared this month's study. She has been summarizing the previous two meetings, and we come in at the end of her comments.

1    MRS. M  So it seems that the Sermon on the Mount is a statement of what all Christians ought to be. It's not a list of 'do's and dont's' for us to live by in order to become Christians, as a lot of people tend to think. Rather, it's a picture of the Christian character, and because we have

# CHURCH FELLOWSHIP

Sample 4

## METHOD

# 3

## KEY QUESTIONS

1   It is helpful to give a summary of the earlier meetings in the series, especially when they are as widely spaced as these. The summary is brief and clear – a lengthy, opening monologue tends to have a soporific rather than a stimulating effect!

Mrs. Marston allows for the fact that not all members of the group are necessarily committed Christians, but wisely refrains from labouring the point.

The use of the rhetorical question has the effect of focusing the attention of the group if their minds should happen to have wandered during the introduction.

become Christians (if we have) this is how we should be living. I think someone commented last time that the Beatitudes are the Christian character in essence, didn't they? Today's passage gives us particular examples, starting at verse 11.

2  MISS C  But what about verse 10? We didn't really deal with it properly last time, did we? I think we ought to look at it again.

3  MRS. M  Yes, perhaps we should. What would people like to say about it?

4  MISS C  Well, I think we tend to think of persecution just as things like being thrown to the lions, but there is still persecution in the world today, isn't there? And even in England, you get people being overlooked for promotion because they won't go for a drink with the boss, and that sort of thing.

5  MRS. B (shocked)  Oh, but surely that doesn't happen?

6  MR. W (sharply)  Of course it does! There was a case the other day . . .

7  MRS. M (interrupting quickly)  Let's have a look at verse 10 fairly carefully and try to see what it really means. We need to decide what persecution is, and what it means to be persecuted for righteousness' sake, don't we?

8  MISS G  Yes, that's important, isn't it? Sometimes we think we are being persecuted because we are Christians, but it's just that people don't like us because we are being pig-headed, or have a bee in our bonnet about something. Then we feel all martyred and virtuous because people aren't friendly!

9  MR. P  But sometimes we've got to be pig-headed, as you call it, and stand up for our principles. When I was at work they used to have a weekly sweepstake, and every week they came round for the money I told them that it was evil and sinful and the devil's work. The others used to make fun of me, but I know I was right.

10  PAUL  Is that being persecuted for righteousness' sake, though? I see what Miss Griffiths means about bringing it on ourselves, because we have a bee in our bonnet about something which might have nothing to do with what Jesus wants us to do. You might not have been persecuted for righteousness' sake, but more because the other workers didn't like you, Mr. P. We've a boy at school who's always on about pacifism and we're all sick of him and avoid him when we can. But I don't think you could say he was being persecuted for righteousness' sake.

11  MRS. M  Well, then, what does 'for righteousness' mean? We've seen some of the things it doesn't mean, but can we be more specific about what it is?

12  MISS G  I suppose we could say it means suffering at the hands of others through being like Christ.

| 2 | Miss Crawford clearly has something to say about verse 10, but Mrs. M has only prepared from verse 11. What does she do? She may have planned to have a short prayer after her introduction and before the discussion opens. Should she use it at this point? |
|---|---|
| 3 | Mrs. M graciously adapts to the situation and takes her cue from Miss C's remarks. A leader needs to be very composed to take this in her stride at the outset of the meeting — a tense leader would have probably been agitated by it. Her question to the group is not very thought-provoking, but does at least open up the subject. (We must remember that she hadn't prepared this verse.) |
| 4 | A helpful contribution with an example. This is always useful in that it particularizes and clarifies a comment. |
| 5–6 | The makings of an argument. The leader must act immediately. |
| 7 | Mrs. M skilfully curtails the developing argument by taking the group back to the verse to establish exactly what is being said there. This takes the contestants' minds off their own thoughts and feelings and gets them thinking positively about something else. A definition at this stage will be helpful before more opinions are expressed. |
| 8 | A stimulating and practical comment, although it suggests what persecution is not, rather than what it is, as requested. |
| 9 | Mr. P goes off at a tangent. His comment in no way helps the group towards a definition, and his attitude could lead to friction. Leader, beware! |
| 10 | A group member questions the relevance of Mr. P's remarks to the question under discussion. This is better than the leader jumping in immediately to question it, although it would have been her responsibility if no one else had. However, Paul's further remarks and illustration are fuel for the fire and the danger increases! Storm clouds are looming, and Mrs. M will need all her skill and tact to avoid real friction. |
| 11 | It is helpful to repeat the request for a definition, and Mrs. M takes the opportunity when the key phrase 'persecuted for righteousness' sake' is repeated by Paul. |
| 12 | Good and helpful. Mrs. M must feel rather relieved, as she may not have had a definition up her sleeve, not having prepared this verse! |

13 MRS. M   That's helpful, thank you, Mary. Being righteous is being like Christ. What do others think of that? Mrs. Peters, does that seem a good way of putting it?

14 MRS. P   Yes, I like that. It's nice to think that we can be like Him.

15 MRS. W   It's a particularly apt definition in view of the fact that Jesus wasn't disliked for anything imperfect in His character. His attitudes and behaviour were always exemplary, so that He was the epitome of righteousness. (Brief pause.)

16 MRS. M   So you are saying the same as Mary, really – that we suffer for righteousness' sake when we suffer because we are acting as He would have done?

17 MR. W   Well, yes, I suppose you could put it like that.

18 MISS G   If we are punished for doing wrong in some way, then that's a different thing altogether, isn't it? Jesus wasn't punished for doing wrong – He was so good that people were shown up by Him, and they didn't like it, so they killed Him. That's 'being persecuted for righteousness' sake'.

19 MISS C   Verses 11 and 12 go into more detail about it, don't they?

20 MRS. M   (relieved)   Let's read them and have a closer look, then. Penny, I see you have Today's English Version. Will you read verses 11 and 12 for us, please? (Penny reads). Thank you.

21 MR. P   (gruffly)   That's not the Bible. (To Penny.) What were you reading?

22 PENNY   (enthusiastically)   It's a modern translation. Everyone at school has got one – even people who don't care tuppence for God or the Church. It's ever so easy to understand.

23 MR. P   It's the devil's work, that's what it is. Shouldn't be allowed. This (pointing to the AV) is the Bible, God's Word. Don't hold with these modern ideas.

24 MRS. M   Some people find the language of the Authorized Version very difficult to understand, Mr. Peters. Perhaps we should ask Mr. Tilney to talk to us one week about the different versions, and we could compare them and see for ourselves. Anyway, we'll move on now and look at the verses Penny read so clearly for us.
(The meeting proceeds . . .
A quarter of an hour later.)

25 MRS. M   a. That seems to have exhausted those verses, so we'll do 13–16.
b. Now, as time is getting on, I've asked Susan to read this for us in the New English Bible. Thank you, Susan (Susan reads). These
c. verses are about the Christian in the world. We are all in the world, and we can't contract out,

13    It is good to show appreciation of helpful comments, as it encourages the contributor and gives confidence to others. It can be embarrassing to have one's remark apparently ignored, and can deter one from making further comment.

Mrs. Peters' only contribution until now has been squashed by Mr. Waters, and this may have prevented her from venturing another comment. A simple question addressed to her personally may help to restore her confidence.

14    Without encouragement, she would not have spoken, and her contribution, though a little naïve, underlines the definition offered by Miss G.

15    The pomposity of this speech silences the group.

16    Mrs. M skilfully translates into simple terms, and breaks the silence.

18    A helpful comment.

19–20    Mrs. M readily agrees to move on. If Miss C had not looked on to the next verses, Mrs. M should have been prepared to do so at about this stage, in order to keep the discussion moving, and to complete the study in the time available.

Note how she draws in the youngest member by giving her something to read and repeating exactly which verses she wants reading. Once Penny has heard her own voice, she is more likely to use it again. Note again the courteous 'Thank you'.

21    A red herring!

22–23    A basic difference in outlook is apparent, but not on an issue relevant to the discussion in hand. A tricky situation for a leader.

24    Mrs. M tactfully tries to calm down the indignant Mr. P without taking sides in the disagreement. She effectively stops the discussion on the issue by suggesting a special meeting where the subject can be properly dealt with. This is better than digressing during the present meeting.

Another useful method in dealing with 'red herrings' is to have a question box on display for questions to be discussed later. A special meeting can be arranged for this, or a panel of experts can be brought in to answer any questions which are beyond the scope of the group.

By commenting on the way Penny read the passage, Mrs. M does all she can to restore any lost confidence.

She firmly but politely steers the discussion back to what is relevant, and has probably averted any ill-feeling.

except by becoming monks or nuns, and that's probably not what God intends us to be. So let's see how we are meant to behave and to be, as Christians in the world.

d. I've written out some questions on bits of paper, and if you will take one as they come round, you can think about them for a minute or so, and look again at the passage. Then I'll be asking you to discuss it for a couple of minutes with the person next to you. (Penny, will you change places with Mr. Waters, then the pairs will be more evenly balanced.) After that we will all share our findings and see what conclusions we can reach. Have you all got a slip of paper now? These are the key questions to the understanding of these verses, so we'll each look at them silently for a minute before we discuss them with our neighbour.

26 *Sample of slips of paper handed out.*
What is the function of salt?
What is the function of light?
What is implied about the world?
How can we apply to ourselves the teaching on salt and light?

27 The meeting proceeds.

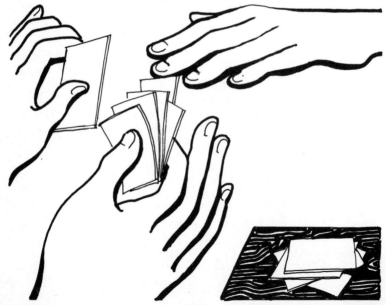

25   a. Mrs. M has her eye on the clock and is keeping to a time schedule.
     b. Susan is young and has been asked in advance to be prepared to read this passage. As everyone now knows that Susan had been given warning of this, no one need fear being pounced on on another occasion – this being something which can prevent shy newcomers from attending a second meeting.
     c. The brief explanation of the content of the passage is useful in helping to clarify in the minds of the hearers the subject matter they are about to deal with, and to put it into context.
     d. The method Mrs. M adopts has several advantages: 1. People can concentrate more easily on a question to which they can keep referring. 2. They can formulate and modify their views in a one-to-one conversation before committing themselves to the larger group. This (a) gives them confidence to express themselves in the larger group and (b) may prevent them from making unconsidered statements later. 3. They can find suitable words with which to express their views and practise them on their partner. 4. Everyone has to participate and think out answers. It would be far too embarrassing to sit and look in silence at one another for two whole minutes, and even naturally quiet members will converse in this situation.

     The method is explained simply and clearly by Mrs. M and at the end she reminds them of what they have to do first. She has seen that in one move she can allocate the partners in the most helpful way possible.

     This is a particularly useful method in a group where there are several potentially silent members, or where people do not yet know each other. Where there is a lot of ground to cover, different pairs can do the preliminary work on different aspects of the subject.

26   The questions used here get to the heart of the meaning and application of these familiar verses.

27   We leave them to their discussion, confident that it will be profitable.

# 6th FORM
## Details

Weekly meeting in the lunch hour at Oxenhurst Comprehensive School. Speakers alternate with Bible studies or discussions, and this week a Bible study is to be led by Mark, the leader of the group. There are usually 6 or 8 members at Bible studies, up to 15 at discussions, and occasionally as many as 30 at meetings with an interesting speaker. All members are aged 16–18.

## Regular members

MARK           *Leader.*
SALLY          *Secretary of the Christian Fellowship.*
HELEN          *Studious and quiet.*
PETER          *Assistant Secretary.*
ROY            *Publicity Secretary.*
JANE           *Roy's girl friend; recently became a Christian.*
ANDREW         *An avowed atheist who attends most meetings.*

Also at this meeting:
TIMOTHY
GRAHAM
DAVID
ALISON
NICOLA

It is 12.30 in the Upper Sixth Form room. Present are Mark, Sally, Peter, Roy, Jane and Andrew.

1    MARK    Everybody here? I thought there might have been more of us. You did give in a notice for assembly, did you, Roy? I was late this morning so I didn't hear it. You did? Good. Mind you, I had a job finding the notice on the Sixth Form board – and it didn't say which room the meeting was in, did it? Do you think anyone might be wandering round looking for us?

2    ANDREW (pleasantly)    Shouldn't think so. Who would be crazy enough to wander round actually looking for a Bible study? I'm only here to show you how wrong you all are!

3    PETER (severely)    That's hardly the right attitude to come with, Andrew. You should be here to learn what God has to say to you.

4    ANDREW    He won't have anything to say to me! He doesn't exist, so how can he?

5    MARK    Let's not have an argument before we start, you two. It's good to see you here again, Andrew, and we'll listen to what you say, only don't forget that we are here to find out what the Bible has to say to us, even if you are not. You had a good innings last week with that visiting speaker, so you'll give us a chance this week, won't you?

# SIXTH FORM CHRISTIAN FELLOWSHIP

Sample 5

### METHOD

### QUESTION AND ANSWER

1    There is no point in planning a meeting unless it is adequately publicized. Announcements should be made where possible, backed up by posters stating clearly the subject matter, the day, time and location of the meeting. However, neither of these methods will be fully effective without the addition of personal invitation.

    Note that Mark was late for school: He may have had a good reason, but if not, the criticism could be levelled against him that his Christian witness is not all it might be.

2    A trouble maker with a pleasant disposition! He will need handling with care.

3    This may not be the most effective way to deal with him, as it will tend to antagonize him.

4    Antagonized!

5    This is the better approach. Mark welcomes Andrew, but shows him clearly where he stands.

6   SALLY   I thought Helen said she was coming. Had we better wait and see if she turns up?

7   MARK   No, I think we ought to start as it's after half past and that leaves us less than half an hour. Has everyone a Bible?

8   PETER   I'll go get one. I'll only be a sec.

9   MARK   You've not got one, Andrew? You can share with Peter when he comes back, then, and Sally can share this one.

(Enter Helen.)

10   HELEN   Sorry I'm late. I was in the library and wasn't sure where the meeting was. Paul said he had looked for you, but he's gone to the chess club because he couldn't find you.

11   JANE   Typical! I knew he wouldn't come when it's a Bible study. People will come to hear speakers, but not to a Bible study. They've no idea what's good for them!

(Re-enter Peter, accompanied by Timothy, Graham, David, Alison and Nicola.)

12   PETER   I met this lot on the way here and when they heard what we were doing they decided to come. I hope that's all right, Mark?

13   MARK   That's fine! (To Jane, aside) Maybe people do realize what is good for them!

14   TIMOTHY (breezily)   We just thought we would drop in and brighten you all up. Holy huddle day, isn't it? Unhealthy, I would say. So here we all are. There's nothing much doing anywhere except the chess club, and they don't let you talk, so we'll ginger you up a bit. Got God sorted out now, have you? Last time I heard, you were having a bit of trouble with his maths — not sure whether there was just one of him, or three.

15   MARK (rather stunned by this attitude)   Well, er, yes, er, come in. We are, er pleased to see you. Have you all got Bibles? (Hurriedly) No, of course not. Well, never mind, you can just listen to us.

(Roy slips out.)

16   GRAHAM   Oh, no, we'll join in, thanks, but we don't need Bibles. A whole load of rubbish!

17   TIM   I'll drink to that!

18   ALISON (in a mock stage whisper)   Careful, Tim, they're probably a temperance lot and they might send you to the devil if they know you actually drink!

19   NICOLA   Oh, cute! What right have they to send us anywhere? We're just as good as them — better, in fact, because at least we are not hypocrites.

20   ANDREW   Well, this *is* a refreshing change! I can see we are in for a lively meeting for once. There's usually only me to liven things up, but it's great to have support!

21   JANE   Come off it! We are here for a serious meeting when

| | |
|---|---|
| 6–7 | It is always a problem deciding whether or not to delay the start of a meeting until all who are expected have arrived. In general, it is probably better to start promptly so that those who are late will have missed part of the meeting and will realize that they will need to be on time in future. If the policy of waiting for everyone is adopted, meetings will tend to start later and later. |
| | Regular members should be encouraged to bring their own Bibles. It is helpful if the leader is able to provide a few additional ones, or, even better, to provide a set of Bibles so that one version may be used as the basis for study and others referred to for comparison. Mark has not come adequately prepared. |
| 8 | Could Peter have gone to collect the one from the lectern in the hall?! |
| 9 | Sharing Bibles is unsatisfactory, as neither party can see the text properly and concentration is impaired. |
| 10 | Better publicity would have tipped the balance here and there would have been one more member present. |
| 14 | Trouble: An influx of several people whose intention is to have fun is more difficult to handle than an unconvinced but sympathetic member like Andrew. Mark is going to need all his skill, and the support of his friends in order to save the meeting. |
| 15 | Mark's reaction is understandable. He is stunned and at a loss for words. His first reaction appears to be to carry on as if the newcomers were not there, but obviously they are not likely to stand for that, and will probably be antagonized at the outset by the suggestion that they can just sit down and listen. |
| 16–20 | They are antagonized! Mark has made a bad start with them. |

we are going to read God's word, not have a slanging match.

22 ALISON  Oh, well, we all know about your sudden interest in religion, Jane! It's surprising how your mind can turn somersaults when you acquire a boy friend!

23 JANE (hotly)  Roy had nothing to do with my conversion, if that's what you mean. God was calling to me to come to Him through Jesus, and that's just what I did. You wouldn't understand!

24 MARK (now more composed)  Now don't start a fight, girls. You said yourself we are not here for a slanging match, Jane. (To the newcomers.) As I said, we are pleased to see you but we have planned a Bible study and we want to hold it.

(Re-enter Roy armed with a set of 'Good News for Modern Man'.)

Here's Roy with some modern translations of the Bible. Did you borrow them from the R.E. Department, Roy? Thanks. If everyone will take one, we'll all use the same version. We are going to look at Colossians Chapter 1, and you'll find that on page, er, let me see, yes, page 449, if you will turn to it, please.

25 NICOLA  I say, you would make a good teacher, Mark! This is just like an English lesson with Old Bossy Guts! 'Open your books and turn to page 449'. Oh, Lord, whatever have we let ourselves in for?

26 ANDREW  Mark's pretty good, Nicola, so you'd better watch it, or he'll have you avidly studying your Bible in next to no time.

27 NICOLA  The trouble with Christians is that they take themselves too seriously.

28 TIM  I'll drink to that!

29 NICOLA (continuing without acknowledging Tim's contribution)  They never seem able to enjoy themselves and go out and have a good time. Why not come to 'The Rave' with us tonight, Mark? We could show you how to have a really super time, and you wouldn't want these stuffy old Bible studies any more. It's a shame for a nice chap like you to miss out on these things.

30 ALISON  Watch it, Nicola — whatever will Tony say?

31 TIM  I'll drink to that! All Bible study and no rave makes Mark a dull boy. That goes for the rest of you, too. How about it, Helen? I bet you've never been to 'The Rave'.

32 HELEN  Certainly not! I wouldn't darken the doors of a sinful place like that night club.

33 GRAHAM  How do you know it's sinful if you've never been? And it's not a night club — it's a coffee bar. You Christians are all the same — you think you're better than everyone else.

34 PETER  We don't think we're better — it's just that we have the Truth, and you haven't.

21–23    Jane perhaps has some sympathy with the newcomers, as she has only recently become a Christian. She tries to be reasonable, but as Alison touches her on a very sensitive point she becomes too worked up to be any help, and the meeting looks doomed to failure.

24    Mark now asserts himself and makes a positive attempt to keep the meeting under control. He is wise to embark on the study as quickly as possible – there is rarely any value in informing a group of any kind that you will start when they are quiet. Their attention needs to be captured in order to silence them, and not vice versa.

Mark is firm and matter-of-fact without being offensive, and he may be able to hold the meeting.

25–36    A digression which Mark should have terminated in its infancy. He is wise to ignore Nicola's mocking of himself, but it is unfortunate that he allows an argument to develop between the group members and the new-comers on a topic which is unrelated to the present study. Once the two groups are lined up against each other, there is a hostile atmosphere and a tendency to one-up-manship which is not conducive to mutually helpful discussion.

A firm line taken by Mark at 29 would have prevented the unpleasantness.

35   ALISON   Good God! Can you beat that for arrogance?

36   DAVID   Come on, let's leave them to their pious talk! — I'm hungry. If we're quick, we'll nick in at the end of first lunch.

37   MARK   You can go if you like, or you are welcome to stay, but we are going to have a Bible study in the quarter of an hour that's left. Page 449 of the TEV. Sally, will you read verses 1 and 2, and Roy 3–8. That's probably all we will have time for. But first Peter is going to pray. Thanks, Peter.

38   ALISON   Good God! How holy!

39   MARK (firmly)   Thanks, Peter.

40   PETER   Dear Lord, please help us all to understand this passage and to believe it. Amen.

    (Sally and Roy read the passage.)

41   MARK   Thanks. The first two verses are the greeting.

42   TIM   Ah, yes! 'Greetings, gentle folk, and all that'. H'm, didn't know they said that sort of thing in those days.

43   MARK (ignoring Tim)   It tells us that the letter is from Paul to God's people in Colossae and he asks God to give them grace and peace. We discussed what that meant when we were studying another epistle, so I think we will leave it for today as time is short.

44   NICOLA   That's pretty speedy. We'll have it all done in a couple of ticks at this rate. Hardly worth coming for.

45   TIM   I'll drink to that!

46   MARK (ignoring them)   The next section is a prayer of thanksgiving, as it says in the TEV.

47   DAVE   He can read, you know.

48   MARK   Paul is grateful to God for the Christians at Colossae and he says he has heard three things about them. What are they?

49   SALLY   The first is their faith in the Lord Jesus, isn't it?

50   MARK   Yes, and what's the next?

51   ROY   Their love for God's people and then, I suppose, their hope.

52   MARK   Yes, that's right. What is the relationship between the faith, love and hope?

    (Slight pause.)

53   GRAHAM   I can't see what you are driving at. I mean, it's all there in the passage, isn't it? Why do you have to analyse it? It seems a pretty useless exercise to me.

54   ANDREW (mysteriously)   Ah well, you see, they've to find out what the secret message is, written between the lines, you know.

55   ALISON   You mean they can't just take it at its face value — they've always got to find some deeper meaning? I once knew a chap like that — he reckoned he got messages straight from God through the Bible. I looked at the same passages and it meant nothing to me. He was suffering

37       Mark is adopting the firm approach and politely proceeds with the meeting in spite of the obvious intention of the newcomers to continue the argument.

What is the best approach in this situation?

In some circumstances, it could be more valuable to abandon the proposed meeting and to concentrate on a subject which will be of interest to the majority. Where, as here, the disruptive element is intent merely on making trouble, and has not come with a specific subject they want to thrash out with the Christians, there would be little value in handing over the meeting to them. Mark is probably adopting the wisest policy here.

38–52   Mark wisely ignores all interjections and at last the meeting is under way. His questions, and the answers they produce, are rather brief but he is leading up to a fuller consideration of the relationship between faith, love and hope and needs to establish the facts first.

from hallucinations, I would say.

56 DAVID I don't know about hallucinations, but I keep getting a mirage with my dinner in the middle of it! Let's go and have some food.

57 TIM I'll drink to that!

58 GRAHAM No, just a minute. I've been looking at this and there's something here I would like to challenge them with. It says here, what I've suspected for a long time, that this famous faith and Christian love they brag about is really just a sham because there's a carrot offered as a bribe.

59 NICOLA Whatever are you on about, Graham? There was nothing about carrots in the thing they read! You're going potty.

60 GRAHAM No! Look, it says, 'Your faith and love are based on what you hope for.' Now what could be plainer than that?

61 DAVID My dinner could! It could be very plain indeed if I just went up into the dining room! Come on, you lot.

62 TIM No, hang on a minute, I see what Graham means. He says the reason they have this faith and so-called Christian love is the pie in the sky that's dangled in front of them. It's a good point, and I think we've got them here, chaps. Now then, you Christians, what do you say to that?

63 SALLY Well, I've never seen pie in the sky dangled before me!

64 DAVID It would probably fall off the plate and wouldn't be any incentive to anyone for anything!

65 MARK Let's not be flippant about it.

66 DAVID Sorry, teacher.

67 JANE (thoughtfully) I didn't become a Christian because of the pie in the sky.

68 ALISON (slyly) No, it was because of Roy, wasn't it?

69 JANE (hotly) It was not! It was because I realized I was a sinner, and I needed a Saviour, and if you clever clogs had any sense you would realize the same! You're all as blind as bats! You think you are so clever, coming and ruining our meeting, but all the time you are sinners needing a Saviour.

70 ALISON (heatedly) I'm not a sinner! I've never been to bed with a boy, and it's not because I haven't been asked. And I can't think why you claim to be so good, Jane Potter. You've a few things to live down before you can call anyone else a sinner!

71 JANE But you don't understand! I *am* a sinner, but I'm saved. I don't claim to be good.

72 MARK Calm down, you two. We are trying to think sensibly about the relationship between faith and love and hope, not to argue about who is the greatest sinner. We are *all* sinners in God's eyes, but He has made a way of salvation for us. Graham has made a good point and I think we

| | |
|---|---|
| 53–57 | Mark cannot prevent a remark such as Graham's but he could perhaps have replied to it promptly, thus forestalling the succeeding unhelpful contributions. He allows the situation to get a little out of hand and appears unable to do anything about it. |
| 58 | This is hopeful! One of the disruptive members is showing interest. If Graham's point can be pursued, some helpful discussion may occur. |
| 59–62 | Nicola is not a help but Graham persists and Tim catches on. Mark should have been involved in this part of the discussion, steering it and throwing it open to the group. However, Tim does this, and the way is clear for an interesting discussion. If the regular group members respond, all may be well. |
| 63 | Oh, Sally! You have let slip a good opportunity of saying something constructive. |
| 65–67 | Mark and Jane are reacting maturely and are prepared to give consideration to Graham's point. This is the right approach. |
| 69–71 | Jane is caught again on this touchy subject and reacts as Alison probably anticipated. Another opportunity slips by and the heated argument and personal vindictiveness draw attention from the original subject. |
| 72 | Mark restores a measure of calm and brings the meeting firmly back to the subject. It is the mark of a good leader to be prepared to give full consideration to a tricky subject. There is always the temptation to shelve such issues, especially in a meeting where there are several unsympathetic members present, but it is wiser to consider such subjects honestly, with a willingness to admit one's own ignorance and to call in expert help where necessary. |

ought to answer it.

73   GRAHAM   Can anyone answer it, then ? I would say that you Christians only have faith and love because of what you hope to get out of it eventually. Isn't that so, if you are honest about it ?

74   ALISON   That figures, because it isn't a real love they have, it's a sham. If it was genuine, they would really care about the poor and the hungry and the homeless. How many of you sold flags last Saturday for the Save the Children Fund ? None, I guess. Good God, they call themselves Christians !

75   HELEN   Now just see here, Alison ! It's not that we didn't want to, it's that most of us had already arranged to go to a day conference and we couldn't withdraw at the last minute, so don't you go accusing us of not caring.

76   ALISON   But Christians are so cold and hard and pious and they never seem to care properly about anyone in need. Oh yes, you talk about love and concern and caring, but you never *do* anything !

77   NICOLA   Except try to stop other people from enjoying themselves.

78   MARK   You've got us all wrong, Nicola. We *do* enjoy ourselves, though perhaps not always in the same way as you do, and we do care about the starving and the homeless. I think you do us an injustice to say ours is a fake love.

79   ALISON   It doesn't seem to show itself in active ways !

80   MARK   (sharply) How do you know ? Have you ever wondered why some of us dash straight out of school at 4.0 while you stay and drink coffee in the common room ?

81   ALISON   No, I can't say I have, and I don't really care.

82   MARK   That's just it, you see. You make these accusations without any evidence.
      (A bell sounds in the distance.)

83   JANE   Until you come to know and love the Lord Jesus, Alison, you won't be able to understand. Why not take my TEV and read it ? You will meet Jesus and begin to realize what Christianity is all about. You need to know that you are not right with God . . .

84   ALISON   Don't go on at me, Jane. I've had enough of you and your evangelistic zeal. We all know you have got it badly but you will grow out of it.

85   TIM   I'll drink to that !

86   ROY   I rather doubt it, Alison, because I haven't grown out of it in ten years.

87   ALISON   You're a bit more reasonable than Jane and some of the others, though, Roy. You don't go around trying to convert everyone. The rest of them are too pious for words !

88   MARK   We're not pious ! We love our Lord and want to serve Him, that's all.

89   NICOLA   Then you're making a pretty poor shot at it !

73–82 Alison is allowed to go off at a tangent and is not brought back to the subject. The responsibility of the leader is to keep the meeting on the subject and, once he becomes heatedly involved in a disagreement, he virtually abdicates the leadership and tends to lose control of the meeting. In the present situation, Mark not only allows the digression to continue and develop into an argument, but he adds fuel to the fire.

83–91 From bad to worse! Mark has lost control of the meeting, and it is brought to a sudden and humiliating end.

90  JANE  That's only your opinion!
        (Enter Sixth Form Master.)
91  SIXTH FORM MASTER  Are you people arguing so loudly
        you can't hear the bell? Don't tell me this is the Christian
        Fellowship? It sounds more like a cattle market! Have
        you forgotten you've to be out of this room now? And if
        you haven't been up to dinner yet, you had better go or
        else you will miss it!
        (Exeunt all, with David muttering about having nearly
        missed his dinner because of these stupid Christians.)

## Post Mortem

What went wrong? What advice would we give to Mark to
help him to deal with a similar situation should it arise?

Mark has the makings of a good leader and has shown that he
knows how to be firm and pleasant. He does not dominate
excessively and is prepared to let others have their say. His
adaptability, demonstrated in his willingness to give full consideration to a point raised by Graham, is commendable, and he
made a valiant attempt to deal with a very difficult situation. If he
had consistently killed the red herrings brought forward by the
troublemakers, and if he had not allowed himself to be drawn into
an argument towards the end, the meeting would have been far
more successful. The point of no return was that at which he
became involved in a heated argument. If at that juncture he
had firmly brought the meeting back to the subject, all would
have been well. Perhaps next time, with the experience of this
meeting behind him, he will do better.

# YOUNG PEOPLE'S FELLOWSHIP
## Details
Weekly meeting after church on Sunday evenings. Age 16–21. It is mid-winter, when numbers at the fellowship are at their peak.

## Members

PAUL — *Leader; last year at school, about to go to University.*
HELEN — *aged 17; studious and quiet.*
BRIDGET — *aged 14; very bright; daughter of vicar; allowed in though under age.*
DAVE — *aged 16; good with hands; training to be car mechanic.*
PATRICIA — *aged 19; librarian; very regular attender; quiet.*
JOHN — *aged 16; talkative and good fun.*
Twenty-four other members.

## Method

Use J. B. Phillips' book of playlets 'A Man Called Jesus' (Fontana), number 21, the death and resurrection of Jesus. Read as a play with the whole group, then discuss and prepare interviews in small groups, reporting back afterwards. N.B. 1. $1\frac{1}{2}$ hours are available in this meeting. In a group with less time available, the session could be continued the following week. N.B. 2. A fairly articulate and intelligent group is needed to use this method.

## At the meeting

1   Paul explains what is about to happen. He then hands out copies of the book, and allocates parts, giving the readers five minutes at this point to read the playlet through. Meanwhile he organizes the members into groups of five or six, each with a leader, and hands to each leader a slip of paper on which are leaders' instructions as follows:

'After the playlet has been read aloud, assemble your group and work for thirty minutes on the assignment asterisked below.
A. Read through the playlet again and list the various aspects of the character of the old soldier, the two thieves, and Nicodemus.
B. Read through the playlet again and prepare an interview between a reporter of the 'Jerusalem Guardian' and the first bystander; the second bystander Sergius, the centurion. The leaders use the remainder of the five minutes to think about their assignment.

2   Read the playlet. This should take about seven minutes. The readers sit in a semi-circle at the front, with the listeners in rows facing them.

If total numbers are less than double the number of readers, everyone sits in a circle, with the readers grouped together in one section of the circle.

3  Groups are formed to work on an assignment according to leader's instructions above. In a large meeting, more than one group could work on each assignment, and in a small meeting the number of assignments can be cut down to suit the group.

We listen in to Group A who have just finished re-reading the playlet quietly.

## Comments on method

This method helps people to think more deeply about the effect of events on the characters involved. The leader of each small group needs to have an imaginative mind, and the general leader should be a good organizer.

1  HELEN (leader of small group)  Let's start with the old soldier and see what we can learn about his character. Who's going to make notes? Will you, Bridget? Thanks. Just make a list of his characteristics as we talk about them and if you want anything repeating, say, won't you?

2  BRIDGET  Does anyone else have to read it? I mean, can I just scrawl it?

3  HELEN  Perhaps if we've time at the end we can make a chart of our findings on this sheet of card for everyone to see, so it doesn't really matter, if no one can read the notes — so long as you can!

4  DAVE  The old soldier doesn't say a lot, does he? I don't see what we can know about him. I think it's a flipping waste of time.

5  HELEN  There doesn't seem to be much, but I think we can work out a bit. At the beginning, what would you say was his attitude to Sergius?

6  PATRICIA  He seems fairly sympathetic to me. After all, he does ask Sergius what's the matter, and has noticed that looks a bit green.

7  JOHN  Yes, and then he goes on to try and jolly him out of it.

8  HELEN  Observant, sympathetic, and helpful to colleagues, then. What about his attitude to Jesus?

9  BRIDGET  He seems worried by Him. Perhaps he suspects that Jesus is innocent — that might be why he's a bit curt with Sergius about it later.

10  HELEN  Yes, that could be. We can say he was made uncomfortable by the presence of Jesus, then.

11  PATRICIA  He's very practical. Have you noticed how he gets on with the job of sharing the clothes? Perhaps a bit greedy, too, because he seems disappointed that there aren't more to share out.

12  JOHN  He's fair, though, and makes them all draw lots for them.

13  HELEN  That seems to be about all on the old soldier. Have

# YOUNG PEOPLE'S FELLOWSHIP
Sample 6

METHOD
6

METHOD
7

DRAMATIZATION          INTERVIEW

1      No messing about. Helen wants to make the best use of the time. She is wise to appoint a scribe at the beginning and not to wait until the end to ask someone to prepare a summary. It is helpful to give detailed instructions of what is expected from the scribe, and to give opportunity to clarify points as they arise.

2      Bridget needs more clarification.

3      Helen has wisely thought this out and even come prepared with a sheet of card on which to make a chart. Visual aids of this simple kind can save time in reporting back and are more easily understood and better remembered than a droning report.

4      Dave is prepared to give up before he starts! How does a leader cope with this?

5      Helen is sympathetic but firm and immediately points the way to the first answer. A specific question is often more effective than a general one to get a discussion going. Once people start talking they are more likely to continue. If the first question is vague and difficult, the resulting silence can embarrass and inhibit the group for the rest of the meeting.

6–7    Short, positive answers.

8      The leader does not acknowledge these contributions, but summarizes them for the benefit of the scribe. Helpful for the scribe, but not good for the confidence of the contributors. A brief 'thank you' would have been appropriate.

9–10  Helen responds well here and makes a further point.

11–12  These two have been studying the text, and make helpful comments.

you got all that down, Bridget?

14 BRIDGET Yes, thanks. Observant, sympathetic, helpful to colleagues, uncomfortable in the presence of Jesus, practical, greedy and fair-minded. Whew, I never thought we would get all that!

15 HELEN Let's compare the two thieves, now. Dave, what can you say about the first thief? Do you think he was being reasonable?

16 DAVE No, I don't.

17 HELEN Why not?

18 DAVE Well, he wasn't, was he?

19 HELEN You can understand that he felt a bit peeved, though, can't you. I mean, he was in agony and about to die a most horrible death, so he couldn't help being a bit upset. And if he thought Jesus could save them, and wouldn't, he had every reason to get all worked up about it. Don't you think so?

20 DAVE (sullenly) Yes, I suppose so. This all seems a waste of time to me — why can't we just read the play and leave it at that? It's like flipping school, doing all this!

21 PATRICIA Never mind, Dave, it'll be coffee-time soon.

22 HELEN What does anyone else think?

23 BRIDGET He was bitter. Even if he had done wrong, it's easy to see why he got so annoyed. People don't always think what they are saying in that situation, I shouldn't think.

24 PATRICIA The other thief was in the same situation, though, and he didn't blame anyone for it, except himself.

25 BRIDGET It's interesting that he accuses the other one of not being able to tell right from wrong. He could see that he was wrong, but that Jesus had never done anything wrong. I think that's great when you think of the pain he was in. I like him!

26 HELEN Let's try to list the differences between them, then.
The discussion continues . . .

| 13 | Contributions again unacknowledged, but Helen is conscious of the passing of time. |
|----|----|
| 15 | Dave has said nothing since his pessimistic opening! Helen tries to bring him into the discussion, first with a general question, and then with a specific one which he could easily answer briefly. |
| 16 | Helen has problems here! |
| 17 | She asks a further question and when there is little response (18) she (19) pursues the subject and makes fairly provocative remarks to try to make Dave say something. |
| 20 | Still no response. Helen is making no headway with the conversation, and she can either abandon it, or pursue it. |
| 22 | She wisely chooses to abandon it as it does not look as if Dave is likely to make any useful contribution. |
| 23–25 | Helpful remarks, and Helen leaves them to it. Unobtrusiveness is a sign of good leadership. |
| 26 | Good. The points have been made and Helen now tries to get a summary for the chart. |

*Later* Group E are presenting the interview they have prepared, between a reporter of the 'Jerusalem Guardian' and the Centurion.

1  REPORTER  I understand that you were actually at the crucifixion of this man Jesus of Nazareth?

2  CENTURION  Yes, I was there.

3  R  Did anything strike you as unusual about him?

4  C  Yes, several things. For one thing, he had an air of determination that you don't often see around men being crucified.

5  R  Have you seen many?

6  C  Hundreds of them, and they either rant and rave, or scream with the pain or just look utterly worn and defeated. But this man didn't do any of those things.

7  R  You were heard to say at the end that he spoke as if he had won a victory.

8  C  (startled)  Oh, they heard me, did they? Yes, well, that was the feeling I had at the time. As if he had done what he had set out to do, somehow.

9  R  Over his head there was an inscription. What did it say?

10  C  The King of the Jews. Pilate had it put there. A dangerous thing to do, I would say.

11  R  Do you think that perhaps he might have been the King of the Jews? After all, you have just said that he seemed to have won a victory.

12  C  Oh, no, I wouldn't go so far as to say that. In fact, it was really the Jews who got him put to death you know, so he couldn't have been their King, could he? And I certainly don't want you to report me as saying he was a King of any sort — that's more than my job's worth! But I can safely say that there was something different about him.

13  R  Would you say you admired him for what he did, and the way he died?

14  C  Yes, I think I would.

15  R  So you don't think he should have been crucified?

16  C  (quickly) I didn't say that!

17  R  They say something unusual happened when he died.

18  C  There seemed to be a sort of earthquake and a crack of thunder, and before that everything had been dark for a long time. The men were frightened and, frankly, I didn't blame them.

19  R  Do you think it could have been the God of the Jew who caused it?

The interview continues.

# General remarks

The interview is well prepared and shows a great deal of thought. The questions of the reporter are brief and clear, and the centurion reacts as might be expected: he shows a certain amount of fear of the authorities, and is not always prepared to commit himself fully in his answers, although he was clearly impressed by the crucifixion.

1   The general question establishing this basic fact is a good beginning. It probably took the group a long time to think out the opening question, which is an important one.

3   A leading question giving the centurion an opportunity to broach any aspect of the crucifixion which impressed him in any way.

4   The reporter does not find out what the other things were – perhaps an opportunity missed.

5   A question to establish the validity of the centurion's comparison.

7   Not a question, but a statement which elicits an immediate response and reveals more about the centurion than a straight question would have done.

The questions and answers gradually build up a picture of what happened, how the centurion reacted at the time, and his present more cautious feelings about it all. Any group could be congratulated on preparing and presenting an interview of this calibre in half an hour.

# THE MIDGETS
## Details
A weekly Bible class for 10–13 year olds and led by a church member and held in his home. The meetings are held on Mondays in the early evening.

## Members

| | |
|---|---|
| MR. MASON | *Leader; middle-aged; married, two sons.* |
| PETER | *13 years.* |
| LORNA | *12 years.* |
| SAMANTHA | *12 years.* |
| DINAH-JANE | *12 years.* |
| DAVE | *12 years.* |
| ANDREW | *11 years.* |
| GRAHAM | *10 years.* |
| STEVEN | *10 years.* |
| ANNE | *10 years.* |

## Methods
Word race team game, and dialogue.

## Text
The young people have assembled in Mr. Mason's front room, which is conveniently large.

1    MR. M    Has everyone remembered a Bible this week? Most of you? Good. I've got a few spare ones here for those without one.

2    LORNA    Can I have one of yours, Mr. Mason, because I can't understand this one.

3    MR. M    Certainly, Lorna. Yours is in old-fashioned English, isn't it? Here is a modern translation. Does anyone else want to exchange for a newer one? Here you are, then. Some of you might like to think about asking for a New English Bible for Christmas, or a Revised Standard Version, or a Good News for Modern Man. I'll show you some of them afterwards, and you can think about it. I can get them for you if your parents agree.

Now, who knows where to find the Acts of the Apostles?

4    SAMANTHA    After the gospels, isn't it?

5    MR. M    That's right. Will you all find it, please. We want Chapter 9 today. Look up when you have found the place, and then I will know when to begin.

Remember that if you have a Bible with Old and New Testaments, the New Testament starts about two-thirds of the way through, so you can turn to it straight away. There are the four gospels, then the Acts of the Apostles, and we want Chapter 9.

# MIDGETS (aged 10–13)
Sample 7

## METHOD

### DIALOGUE

## METHOD

### TEAM GAME

## Details

Home meetings on weekdays tend to have a better attendance in some areas than Sunday Bible classes. This may be because a weeknight meeting seems more adult than Sunday school.

## Members

There may be problems because of the age range. A 13 year old may find some of the 10 year olds' activities rather childish.

## Methods

The word race is described in the text. For dialogue see Method 8 on page 28

1      Spare Bibles are essential to ensure that everyone has a copy during the meeting. At least one member is likely to have forgotten this copy in a group like this one. In some groups, a points system is adopted where each member earns a point for his team if he remembers his Bible, brings a friend, etc. Different groups react in different ways to this kind of system. I was once firmly rebuked by a sincere 12 year old who felt that such 'bribery' was quite unethical!

3      Modern translations are a big help. If children – and older people, too – become familiar with them, they are likely to want to own one for themselves. Mr. M makes it as easy as possible for the members of his group to acquire one, by offering to purchase the Bibles on their behalf.

5      Mr. M is helping them to find Acts in their own time, and to be able to find it again. He keeps talking until he has seen that everyone has found it! It can be humiliating to be the last to find a passage!

6　ANDREW　We're not reading all of it, are we?

7　MR. M　No, Andrew, just the first 30 verses!

8　ANDREW　We'll be here all night!

9　PETER　Oh, shut up, Andrew. You needn't have come if you didn't want to.

10　MR. M　I think you'll find it quite interesting, Andrew. It's about a chap who was a bit like you — forceful and determined with a strong personality. In fact, he spent a long time working very enthusiastically trying to stamp out something he thought was wrong. Then something dramatic happened, and he changed his mind about it all.

11　GRAHAM　It's Saul of Tarsus, isn't it?

12　MR. M　That's the man, Graham. Have you heard about him at school? What did he do?

13　GRAHAM　Yes. He persecuted the Christians, but then he was converted and became a missionary.

14a　MR. M　That's right. Let's read about it and fill in a few more details. How many of you would like to read today? Right, if you read verses 1–9, Lorna, you 10–16, Samantha, and you 17–19, Dave. There will be some more to read later. Fire ahead, and the rest of you follow it in your own Bibles.

　　　(The passage is read.)

14b　Will anyone tell us in a couple of sentences what happened?

15　PETER　Well, Saul was going to Damascus to arrest the Christians, but he met Jesus on the way and became blind. Then God told this other man to go to him and he did and Saul could see again.

16　MR. M　Thanks, Peter. Who has a question to ask?

17　LORNA　Why didn't the other people see Jesus?

18　MR. M　That's a difficult one. I think Jesus must have wanted just Saul to see Him, so He only appeared to him, but I don't know how, really.

19　STEVEN　What does it mean about these scales falling from his eyes? Seems a bit silly to me — big things like that on his eyes.

20　SAMANTHA　It doesn't mean scales that you use for weighing, you dope — it's like fish scales, isn't it, Mr. Mason?

21　MR. M　(laughing) Yes, that's right, Samantha, but it doesn't make it very clear here, so we can't blame Steven for not understanding just at first.

　　　It was Saul's way of explaining what happened to him. Any other questions? You do realize that Saul is Paul, don't you? Saul was his name before conversion, but afterwards he was always known as Paul.

22　DAVE　Oh, I see! So he's the chap who had all those missionary journeys they are always doing at school? I thought he was just born as a fully-grown missionary. Fancy him not being a Christian at first!

6–10    Andrew is unco-operative, but Mr. M wisely talks to him in pleasant tones, slipping in an encouraging compliment, and makes the prospective study sound exciting.

Unco-operative group members can be a menace, and can undermine the enthusiasm and responsiveness of the whole group, but there is no infallible way of dealing with them. If the situation becomes impossible, and one member is ruining the meeting, it may be advisable to send him home, but this must be a last resort, as he is unlikely ever to return. Persistent pleasantness on the part of the leader will occasionally work. Or the problem may be solved by pointing out the individual's responsibility to other group members, or by giving him a specific task to absorb his extra energy!

11, 14a    Graham's attention is gained, and he is delighted to share his knowledge. It can be useful to give a few clues on the subject matter to bring out the detective instincts in the group, who immediately feel involved in what is going on. Mr. M asks for volunteers for reading, and does not compel anyone to read who shows a disinclination for it.

14b–22    Mr. M believes in giving the group plenty of opportunity to ask questions. This is excellent, as it can prevent misconceptions from arising, and can clear up issues which are somewhat cloudy in people's minds. Because Mr. M expects them to ask questions, they will do so — this is far more satisfactory than members having to interrupt in order to clarify a point. Young people in particular are unlikely to ask in case they are alone in their ignorance.

Note that Mr. M. does not ridicule Steven for asking a silly question — scorn and ridicule will stifle further questions.

125

23    MR. M   Any more questions? I want you to divide into two teams, then — one over here and one over there. Peter, you can be a supervisor in the middle here by the table. That's right, pull your stools across. On this table in the middle there are two sets of 15 cards, one set for each team.

24    ANNE   Is it one of those races again, Mr. Mason? I like those.

25    MR. M   Yes, it is, Anne. It's fun, and it helps us all to look hard at the passage and get to know it. Each card has a word from the passage written on it, but they are all jumbled up, so I want you to set them out on the floor in the order in which they occur. One person at a time comes out for a card, and when he has got back to his group, someone else comes and collects another one, while the rest of the group place the first card. Decide who is running first and what order the rest are coming in. All set? Peter will check that you collect your cards from the right pile, and that you collect only one at a time. Right, off you go.

      (Noise and bustle follow. After three minutes, team A has all the words in the right order. While Mr. M checks the order, team B finishes.)

26    MR. M   Whew! I'm quite tired watching you do all that rushing about! We should all know the story pretty thoroughly now. Are there any questions? No? Let's read verses 19–30 next. Any offers? I'll read it then.

      (He reads.)

      What questions do you want to ask from this?

27    ANNE   Why did the Jews want to kill him?

28    MR. M   Does anyone else know?

29    PETER   It was because he was getting some converts from the Jews, wasn't it?

30    MR. M   Yes, partly, and because he was claiming that Jesus was the Messiah the Jews were waiting for. Most of them didn't believe that.

31    ANNE   They must have had very big baskets, for him to have got into one!

32    ANDREW   I think Saul or Paul or whoever he was was a coward. You wouldn't get James Bond running away like that. It's a bit soft to be let out of a window in a shopping basket!

33    MR. M (pleasantly), Perhaps you have a point there, Andrew. But we need to remember that he wouldn't have stood a chance if he had gone out of one of the gates, because the Jews were waiting there to ambush him. Perhaps he wanted to get away at any cost, so that he could carry on with his preaching somewhere else. I think if you read more about him, you'll find that he certainly wasn't frightened of getting into a jam. Perhaps you would each like to find out for next week one of the brave things he did after this. It's all in the Acts.

23–25   Mr. M explains the method clearly, leaving no doubt in the group's minds as to what is expected of them. He wisely gives a special task to Peter who, being older than the others, may find their activities beneath his dignity.

26      In the absence of offers to read, Mr. M does it himself. This is quicker than trying to persuade someone, and is more likely to produce offers next time.

26–31   Question time again. The young people have no excuse for not understanding the passage.

32–33   Andrew is still in an unhelpful frame of mind, but once more Mr. H is pleasant with him, and offers an explanation, in addition to suggesting something positive that can be done. Perhaps Andrew will refrain from such remarks in the future!

The dialogue method is clearly explained, and the group given a chance to query any point they have not understood.

Now I want you to look back again at verses 26–30, where it says that Barnabas persuaded the other disciples to accept Saul, or Paul as we can now call him. I want you to work out the sort of things he might have said to convince them that Paul was all right. He would tell them all he knew about him and you will find that in the passage we read. Work in threes and decide what sort of things you are going to say. I'll be the spokesman for the disciples, and you can all try to convince me about Paul. Do you all understand? I'll give you about ten minutes to get your ideas sorted out. There are sheets of paper and pencils here if you want to make any notes.

(Ten minutes of general chatter elapse.)

34   MR. M   Everyone ready? We'll have your group starting, Lorna. Remember, I'm frightened that Paul is trying to take all the Christians prisoners, and that we are about to be tricked by him. Each group can have one turn at trying to convince me, and then we'll go back round the groups again for any other arguments you have. Off you go, Lorna and Co.

35   LORNA   We think that Saul, or Paul as he is calling himself, is a real disciple of Jesus. He has been here in Jerusalem for just a short time, but I have talked to him and am sure he is converted. He told me all about the way he persecuted Christians, and how he was going to Damascus to get some more, when he met Jesus Himself. He is very sorry indeed that he arrested so many Christians before, and I think that if you talk to him, you will believe him.

36   MR. M   I don't want to see him, because he might take my name and report me to the authorities and have me arrested.

37   SAMANTHA   No, I'm sure he will not do that, because he hasn't had anyone arrested since he became a Christian, and that shows that he is a real Christian.

38   MR. M   He might just be waiting until he has collected as many names as he can before he reports everyone.

39   DINAH-JANE   No, he is so sorry about the ones he did arrest, that you can't help believing him. And when he tells you about how Jesus met him and talked to him, he'll convince you. He told me that there was a sudden flash of light, and a voice asked him why he was persecuting Him, and said that He was Jesus. Then Jesus told him to go on to Damascus and to wait there.

40   DAVE   Yes, and Ananias went to see him, and he saw him get his sight back, and receive the Holy Spirit.

41   MR. M   But all this might be a trick on us. Have you any proof that he means what he says?

42   STEVEN   He has preached about Jesus in the synagogues in Damascus, and tried to win converts. He wouldn't do that if he wasn't on our side, would he?

34–42 The role-play develops as planned, with Mr. M giving a good lead.

(The discussion continues.)
Later.

43   MR. M  You have convinced me! We will welcome Paul among the apostles, because he has seen the risen Lord.

      You have done very well, thank you very much. Remember to see if for next week you can find one example of Paul being brave.

      Is there anything you would specially like us to pray about this week?

44   GRAHAM  My grandma is in hospital and my mum is worried a lot.

45   MR. M  We will certainly pray for your grandma, and the whole family, Graham.

46   PETER  I've got a music exam on Thursday.

47   MR. M  We will pray that you will do your best then, Peter. Is there anyone else? Let's pray, then, and if you think of anything I do not mention, you talk to God about it in the silence at the end.

43–47 Mr. M gives credit where he feels it is due. It is always encouraging to be complimented on what we have done, and a leader should give constant encouragement. It is a good idea for young people to begin to offer prayer for other people and for situations in which they find themselves. Corporate prayer of this kind can help to develop their private prayer life, as well as being very valuable in itself.

This has been a good, well-led, and interesting meeting. The members will now be familiar with the story of Paul's conversion, and will have a clear idea of the difficulty the Christians in Jerusalem had in accepting Paul.

# SECTION 3 OUTLINES
## CONTENTS

# Part A
FULL OUTLINES

page

# Part B

Fifty-two brief outlines from the Old and
New Testaments
Suggestions for meetings using the case
history or Topical Study method
Suggestions for meetings using audio
and visual aids
Suggestions for meetings using the
Character Study method

See also 'Note on Use of Appendices' for guidance on materials
and methods for further meetings.

## Full outlines   Set one

| | | |
|---|---|---|
| 1 | The Perfect Man | A study on the character of Jesus Christ |
| 2 | What's Wrong With Me? | A study on sin |
| 3 | Failure or Success? | A study on the death of Jesus Christ |
| 4 | Man Alive! | A study on the Resurrection of Jesus Christ |
| 5 | Becoming a Christian | A study on conversion |
| 6 | Men Alive! | A study of the early church |
| 7 | How to Win Friends | A study on personal relationships |
| 8 | For Christ's Sake | A study on Christian suffering |
| 9 | Where is Love? | A study on neighbourly love |
| 10 | Till Death Us Do Part | A study on Christian marriage |
| 11 | What's Wrong with the World? | A study on social evils |

# Introductions to full outlines (Set one)

The outlines should only be used after the foregoing chapters have been read. The methods suggested are described in section 1, examples of several of the methods are offered in section 2, and sundry hints are to be found in the introductory section and in the appendices.

The outlines form a series on basic Christian doctrine and practice suitable for a group of older teenagers, but adaptable for a wider age range.

Each outline is developed by a different method in order to give variety of presentation, and to introduce methods which may then be used when studying other passages.

The Biblical references throughout are to the Revised Standard Version.

# OUTLINE 1

## THE PERFECT MAN
## A study on the character of Jesus

## Method to be used

Character study using chart.

## Equipment

Bibles (passage to be studied – John 4. 1–42).
Large sheet of paper/blackboard.
Felt pen/chalk.
Map of Palestine, or sheet of paper and pen for making one.

## Notes for leader

1   Read Method 12 (p. 39  and following) on use of character study method.
2   Prepare simple sketch as follows.

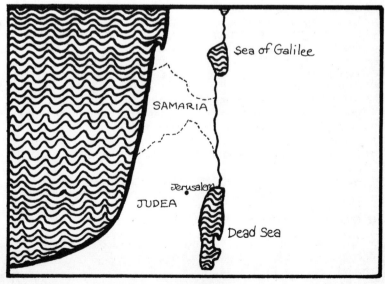

# Presentation to the group

1 Introduction.
   We are going to make a character study of Jesus based on an incident in John's gospel, chapter 4, when Jesus met and talked with a Samaritan woman. It is in some ways surprising that Jesus talked to her, because the Samaritans and the Jews had fallen out. It all began in the 8th century before Christ, when the Northern Kingdom of Israel was conquered by the Assyrians, and most of the people were exiled. Later, Judah was conquered and exiled to Babylon. A few stayed behind, and they were joined by exiles from other nations conquered by the Assyrians. They all lived together, and became known as the Samaritan nation. When the Israelites came back from exile in Babylon they would have nothing to do with the Samaritans, because they felt they were not true Israelites, having intermarried with foreigners. From that time onwards, the Israelites and the Samaritans were enemies.

   In spite of this, Jesus talked to a Samaritan; and not only to a Samaritan, but to a woman. Jewish men despised women – in fact a prayer they used regularly said 'Blessed art thou, O Lord . . . who hast not made me a woman'! So it is from this surprising incident that we are going to see how much we can learn about the character of Jesus.

2 Read, taking parts – narrator, Jesus, woman, disciples, Samaritans. (N.B. The narrator should read the whole of verses 27 and 39.)

3 Leader, briefly summarize the story.

4 Show the map (see notes for leader), and indicate the general route Jesus took. (N.B. Most Jews went round Samaria, but Jesus chose to go through it.)

5 Divide into small groups and allocate a section of the passage to each group. Ask them to list as many aspects of the character of Jesus as can be found.

6 Any questions? N.B. v. 20 'this mountain' is Mt. Gerizim, the sacred mountain of the Samaritans, on which was a temple.

7 After a suitable length of time (5–10 minutes), reassemble the groups and, working systematically through the passage, list the findings on chart or board. After each section has been completed, ask the whole group to add any points to those already suggested.

8 Discuss the findings, and deal with any questions which arise.

9 Summarize the findings, if possible grouping together related aspects of the character of Jesus, and emphasizing His humanity and divinity.

10 Close in prayer, thanking God for the perfect character and example of Jesus.

# OUTLINE 2

## WHAT'S WRONG WITH ME?

### A study on sin

### Methods to be used

Newspaper and magazine cuttings; Question and answer; Chart.

### Equipment

Sheet of paper/blackboard for wall chart.
Felt pen/chalk.
Cuttings from newspapers and magazines.
Bibles (passages to be studied:
   Genesis 3. 1–7, 22–24
   Matt. 23. 34–39
   Romans 5. 6–8
   Luke 13, 1–5)

### Notes for Leader

1 Read Method 11 (page 33 and following) for use of visual aids and Method 1 (page 16 and following) for Question and Answer.

2 Find and cut out from newspapers and magazines reports, articles, etc. which illustrate the existence of sin and evil in the world. Take care to select not only cuttings which relate to the more spectacular sins (e.g. reports on war and violence, and of quarrels leading to divorce action) but also, e.g. letters from problem pages of women's magazines which illustrate the feelings of moral failure and inadequacy on the part of ordinary people.

3 Prepare a chart as follows and fasten it up where it can be seen.

*What's Wrong?*
Where did the trouble start?
What was the result?
Who is guilty?
The remedy?
Our response?

4 In the introduction to this study, it will be particularly important not to be, or appear to be, superficial. For example, a true understanding of the Biblical doctrine of sin will not lead us totally to deny that environments can influence character, nor to deny the value of some forms of legislation in keeping evil within bounds.

# Presentation to the group

1   Give a brief explanation of the mechanics of the meeting – a look at press cuttings, to be followed by discussion and a Bible study.
2   Open in prayer, if appropriate for your group.
3   Display the press cuttings, and if possible get members of the group to read different extracts from them.
4   Ask the group questions along these lines:

'What kind of explanations do people give as to why there is so much evil and moral failure in the world?' 'How do we ourselves explain this?'

Allow some minutes for free exchanges of ideas here, bearing in mind that (see note above) group members may quite rightly assert that, e.g. overcrowded or slum housing conditions may lead teenagers into vandalism, though the Christian would also point out both the universal bias towards sin and the fact that bad housing conditions were the result of the sinful greed of landlords or the equally sinful selfishness of voters at election time.

5   Introduce the Bible study by saying that we are going to look at what Christians believe to be the origin and root cause of evil in the world, and at how what the Bible calls sin began. Explain that it is not proposed to discuss the historicity of the third chapter of Genesis, but rather to extract the main teaching from it.

6   All turn to Genesis, chapter 3, 1–7, and 22–24.

Read – either one person reading the whole passage or, if all have the same translation, have a narrative reading. You will need a narrator and readers for the parts of the serpent and the woman.

God had created Adam and Eve and they were living contentedly in the Garden of Eden, enjoying each other's and God's company. God had given them free will so that they could choose whether to obey Him or not.

What state of mind do you think Adam and Eve were in before the serpent came along?

What would be their state of mind after they disobeyed God? Throughout this passage as a whole, what are the results of sin?

What is sin?

(Leader: draw the group's attention to the chart and fill in the first two sections on the right-hand side.)

Do not dwell too long on this section. Simply establish the following points:

(1)  Adam and Eve were happy when they obeyed God, and unhappy, ashamed, etc. when they disobeyed.
(2)  The main result of sin is separation from God, and this causes dissatisfaction, etc.
(3)  Sin is disobedience against God.

7   All turn to Matthew 23. 34–39. Read.
     How many people, do you think, keep both of these commandments completely?
     Do we keep them? Why not?
     (Leader: If members are not convinced that everyone except Jesus is a sinner, turn up the following references and ask what point is being established:
     Romans 3. 10–12 and 23. If they are still unconvinced, it would be wiser simply to point out that this is the Biblical view and that in this study it is the Biblical view that we are trying to understand. But you should offer them the opportunity to discuss the authority of the Bible on another occasion.)
     Fill in the third section on the chart.

## The remedy

   We find that in the life and death of Jesus Christ, He took our sin on Himself and suffered God's punishment for it.
8   All turn to Romans 5. 6–8. What has God done about sin? Why? Fill in 'The Remedy' on the chart.
9   Salvation – or rescue from sin – is not automatic – we need to make a response to God's love. All turn to Luke 13, 1–5. Read. What response should we make? Fill in the response on the chart.
10  *Conclusion*
     Look again at the chart and summarize the findings.
     The chart should look something like this:

| *What's Wrong?* | |
| --- | --- |
| Where did the trouble start? | Adam and Eve |
| What was the result? | Separation from God, spiritual death, shame, lack of harmony between people |
| Who is guilty? | Everyone |
| The remedy? | The Cross of Jesus |
| Our response? | Repentance |

11  Close in prayer, possibly meditating on the chart summary.

139

# OUTLINE 3

## FAILURE OR SUCCESS?

### A study on the death of Jesus Christ, based on His words from the Cross

### Methods to be used

Group Preparation and Key Questions.

### Equipment

Bibles (passages to study before the meeting:
Matt. 27. 32–54
Mark 15. 16–41
Luke 23. 26–49
John 19)

### Notes for Leader

1   Read Method 16 (page 44 and following) for Group Preparation, and Method 3 (page 19 and following) for Key Questions.
2   Read the passages for study listed above, all footnote Old Testament references, and a good commentary on the gospel passages, with special attention to comments on the words of Jesus from the Cross. (See Bibliography for Commentaries.)

# Presentation to the group

1 Open in prayer.
2 Explain that the meeting will consist of a detailed study of the words of Jesus from the Cross, in the context of the background reading which it is expected that group members will have done, as above.
3 Consider the following questions: (the ones marked * raise particularly profound issues)

Luke 23. 34 'Father, forgive . . . ' What can this teach us about Jesus?

Luke 23. 43 'In Paradise'. What attitude(s) did the thief show which resulted in his being accepted by Jesus? What can we learn from this?

*Matt. 27. 46 'My God, My God . . . ' In the light of Psalm 22, what does this mean?

John 19. 26–27 'Behold your son'. What light does this throw on the love of Jesus for others?

John 19. 28 'I thirst' (ref. to Psalm 69. 21). What do we learn about the humanity of Jesus?

Luke 23. 46 'Into Thy hands . . . ' What can we learn about the relationship between God the Father and God the Son?

*John 19. 30 'It is finished'. What was finished? How? What had been accomplished?

4 Concluding question. Was Christ's death a failure or success?
5 Summarize and close in prayer, perhaps meditating on each of the words from the Cross.

# OUTLINE 4

**MAN ALIVE!**

**A study on the Resurrection of Jesus Christ**

**Method 9**

Newspaper report.

## Equipment

Pens and paper — long strips for reports, large sheets on which to stick reports.

Sellotape.

Bibles (passages to be studied:

Matt. 27. 57 – 28. 20

Luke 24. 1–53

Additional passages to be read beforehand by leader:

Mark 16. 1–20

John 20. 1–23)

## Notes for Leader

1   Read Method 9 (page 29 and following) on Newspaper Report method.
2   Become familiar with accounts in all four gospels (listed above), by reading and re-reading in different translations.
3   It is vital that group members should stick closely to the facts as reported in the gospels, and not make any additions which are inconsistent with the Biblical accounts.
4   (a) Nelson's 'Atlas of the Bible' contains a diagram, a plan, and a picture of a typical Jewish grave, which could be included here.
    (b) If the artist is in difficulties, he could copy two or three of the pictures from the relevant passages in 'Good News for Modern Man'.
5   A subsequent meeting could take the form of a discussion on the implications of the resurrection for us today, considering the fact of the resurrection, the reason for the resurrection and the results of the resurrection.

# Presentation to the group

1   Explain the method – a newspaper account is to be compiled dealing with the various aspects of the Resurrection of Jesus Christ. The newspaper is the 'Jerusalem Echo', and the issue in question is the one for the Monday after Easter Sunday.
2   Opening prayer.
3   Read the account in Matthew (chapter 27. 57 – 28. 20). This may be read aloud by one or more persons, or silently.
4   List (on wall chart, or note pad) assignments.
    The following is a suggested list which you may adapt to suit the needs and capabilities of your group.
    Editor – to read and amend all accounts, eliminate overlap, etc.
    Artist – to sketch selected people and places.
    Reporter – to give a straightforward account of events.
    Reporter – to interview Mary Magdalene (Matt. 28. 1–10).
    Reporter – to interview Joseph of Arimathea (Matt. 27. 57–61).
    Reporter – to interview soldier (Matt. 28. 11–15 plus Matt. 27. 62–66).
    Reporter – to prepare 'Late News Flash' of Emmaus Road incident (from Luke 24. 1–35).
    Compiler of final edition – to assemble the various accounts and attach to large sheets of paper for display. (The Editor may have time to do this.)
5   Re-read silently the Matthew account, and one person (or two) the Luke account.
6   Allocate assignments and briefly discuss what is required in each. (Leader: add names to the assignment list, either on wall chart or note pad.)
7   Distribute paper and pens, and give a specified time for work on assignments, recommending constant reference to text. (Leader: do not take on an assignment, but remain free to give assistance where necessary.)
8   Leader: five minutes before the end of the allotted time, check on progress.
9   Leader: during the last five minutes, see as many accounts as possible and suggest any last-minute alterations.
10  Assemble the accounts, attaching them with Sellotape to larger sheets of paper for display.
11  Close in prayer.

# OUTLINE 5

**BECOMING A CHRISTIAN**

## A study on conversion

## Method 2▦

Basic doctrines.

## Equipment

Bibles – various modern translations, and if possible a set of one translation.

(Passage to be studied – Ephesians Chapter 2.)

## Notes for Leader

1 Read Method 2 (page 18 ) for Basic Doctrines method.
2 v. 1. 'He' – God.
   v. 2. 'prince of the power of the air' – Satan, the devil.
       'sons of disobedience' – people in their natural attitude of disobedience to God.
3 Distribute copies of some translations to everyone (for detailed study of the text), and use as many other translations as possible for the original reading aloud, and for comparison during the study.
4 Some of the questions in section 5 may be covered during the consideration of the questions in section 4, and should not then be mentioned again. The final question in section 5 should be included if the other questions have not resulted in any specific personal comment, and if you feel that it is appropriate.

# Presentation to the group

1 Open in prayer.
2 Introduction.
   This is part of a letter, generally believed to have been written by Paul to churches probably in the Asia Minor area, including Ephesus. The passage is packed with deep thoughts and concepts, and is one in which every word counts. A detailed study is therefore necessary.
3 Read the passage aloud slowly, in two or three different translations.
4 Consider the following questions:
   What is this passage basically about?
   (Being made alive, becoming a Christian, being saved, what God has done, etc.)
   What does the passage teach about man
   (a) before he is a Christian?
   (b) after he has become a Christian?
   What does the passage teach about God the Father, God the Son and God the Holy Spirit?
5 Additional questions:
   What aspects of the past, the present and the future does the passage refer to?
   In what ways is a person dead before he is a Christian, and alive afterwards?
   What is the difference between grace and faith? (v. 8).
   Are people in general aware that there is anything wrong with their lives?
   If not, should we try to tell them, and if so, how?
   Where do good works fit in? (vv. 8–10).
   What does it mean to be saved by grace, through faith?
6 Close with prayers of thanksgiving for what God has done for us.

# OUTLINE 6

## MEN ALIVE!
### A study of the early church
### Method 6

Dramatization and discussion.

## Equipment

Bibles — one set of modern translation (e.g. NEB).
> (Passage to be studied — Acts (2), 3, 4.)
> Note pad and pens.
> Slips of paper.
> Large sheet of paper for chart.
> Felt pen.

## Notes to Leader

1. Read Method 6 (page 23 and following) for dramatization plus Bible Study.
2. If time is limited, omit Acts Chapter 2 and deal only with Chapters 3 and 4, or take two meetings over the study.
3. The division into scenes in Presentation to the group (see below) is only a suggestion, and different divisions may be adopted perfectly satisfactorily.
4. Three to four are usually the most efficient number to have in each group, with one writing the script, one directing the group and working with the other members to decide what should be included.
5. Encourage the groups to summarize long speeches, selecting the vital points only, in order to keep the drama moving.
6. The groups should allocate to the narrator any points not made in direct speech, e.g. chapter 3, verse 4 — (Narrator) 'And Peter directed his gaze at him, with John, and said', (Peter) 'Look at us'.
7. In the allocation of reading parts, involve all members in group speeches, i.e. Jews, hearers, priests, brethren (see list of characters).
8. Write out the questions for discussion (section 4) on slips of paper to be handed to each group for consideration while you look at the scripts.
9. Encourage as many of the group as possible to read through the chapters beforehand.

# Presentation to the group

1  Explain the method – to read and study certain chapters of Acts and dramatize them in scenes.

2  Divide into groups, each with a leader, and allocate section to be studied.

   According to the number of groups, and the sub-division of the passage, each group may take one or more scenes.

   Hand out pens, and note paper headed with the Biblical reference of the section to be studied.

   Each group summarizes in dramatic form the content of its section. Allow a realistic period of time for this, and inform the groups of it, giving warning five minutes before the end.

3  Work in groups.

   During this time, the leader may like to write upon a chart the scene divisions, and a list of characters.

   *Suggested scene divisions*

   Scene 1. Ch. 2. 1–13   Narrator, devout Jews (half of whom read direct speech part of v. 12, half read v. 13).

   Scene 2. Ch. 2. 14–47   Narrator, Peter, 'Hearers'.

   Scene 3. Ch. 3. 1–10   Narrator, Peter.

   Scene 4. Ch. 3. 12 – Ch. 4. 4   Narrator, Peter.

   Scene 5. Ch. 4. 5–22   Narrator, priests, Peter and John.

   Scene 6. Ch. 4. 23–31   Narrator, brethren.

   *List of characters*

   Narrator

   Peter

   John

   Devout Jews

   'Hearers'

   Priests

   Brethren

4  Collect the notes made by each group and sort into chronological order. Modify where necessary.

   Meanwhile, hand out the following questions to be discussed in each group after they have skimmed quickly through the passage :

   Ch. 2. 1–13   What do you think happened ? Does it happen today ? Should it ?

   *Ch. 2. 37–42   Do you think these converts would continue to hold the faith ? If so, why ? If not, why not ?

   *Ch. 3   Peter took any opportunity to preach the gospel. Do such opportunities come to us ? If so, do we use them ? Should we use them and if so, how ?

   Ch. 4   List the characteristics shown by Peter and John in this situation. Would we react in the same way ? What can we learn from them ?

5  Allocate parts and give the group's scripts (modified where necessary) to readers.

   Work through the scenes, omitting long speeches, and

147

ensuring that all readers know when they speak.
6   Take the play reading in full.
7   Briefly discuss answers to questions under section 4 in open group.
8   Close in prayer.

# OUTLINE 7

## HOW TO WIN FRIENDS
## A study on personal relationships

## Method 10◩ 1▓

Topical study, or case history method. Charts, Question and Answer.

## Equipment

Bibles – various translations, including one set of a modern translation. (Passage to be studied – Philippians 2. 1–18.)
Large sheet of paper for chart.
Felt pen.
Flash cards (if required).

## Notes for Leader

1  Read Method 10 (page 31 and following) for Topical Study.
2  The details of the case history will be difficult to remember, and could be written up beforehand on a chart, or duplicated for circulation at the appropriate time.
3  Flash cards may be used for compiling the charted list of the attitudes of the men in the case history. These will have words written on beforehand, and will need attaching to the sheet (see Method 11 on use of AVA). Leave some cards blank for points raised by the group, in addition to the ones you have worked out yourself.

# Presentation to the group

*Stage 1*

1    Describe the following situation:

A well-established firm of breakfast cereal manufacturers is considering setting up a new factory to manufacture an entirely new cereal. The directors of the company have differing views on the advisability of the enterprise, but each has some personal reason for his views.

*The public relations director* is in favour, because he sees it as an opportunity to build up his own department, adding more staff, and thus increasing his own importance.

*The finance director* is not in favour, because he had plans for another new project which his son could have supervised. Only one new project can be launched at a time, and if the original one is undertaken, his son will not have the opportunity to gain promotion.

*The sales director* hopes to use a new advertising gimmick on the new product, in order to win a prize in the 'Best Advertisement of the Year' competition, and is therefore in favour of the project.

*The staff director* sees the new project as extra work for himself, with the need to recruit more staff, train them, etc. He grumbles that this will take longer than the other directors are prepared to give him, and that he always has to put in more hours of work than they do, anyway.

*The export director* sees the new cereal, which is primarily for the home market, as a threat to the export side of the business, and to his own importance, and therefore does not favour it.

*The technical director* insists on heading the investigation team on the basis that there is no one better qualified or more capable than himself. Without him the whole project would fail.

*The managing director* always doubts the wisdom of new enterprises and questions the need for this one. He objects on principle to anyone else's ideas.

2    List the attitudes of these men on a chart. Discuss what is wrong with them.

(Leader: compile the list on the chart yourself and be guided in the phrasing of what you write by the points raised in the Bible passage. Do not make an inaccurate record of the group's views, but by prompting, etc. you can occasionally modify a point, or extract an additional one.)

*Stage 2*

1    Turn to Philippians 2. 1–18.

2    Introduction: The letter was almost certainly written by Paul when he was in prison in Rome about A.D. 64, to the Christians in Philippi.

3    Read verses 1–11 in a modern translation.

Verses 1–5   List the advice Paul gives and then discuss its

150

meaning for today in practical terms. Work in pairs, each pair taking one piece of advice and briefly giving an example of how it can work out in practice.

Share the examples with the full group.

What can we infer about the Christians in Philippi from these verses?

Verses 6–8  List the characteristics of Jesus and discuss their meaning.

Verses 9–11  What is God's purpose in exalting Christ?

4  *Read verses 12–13.*

Put these verses into your own words.

5  *Read verses 14–18.*

Why does Paul tell them not to grumble or question?

*Stage 3*

Leader: briefly re-cap details of case history discussed in Stage 1. In the light of what you have learned from the Bible study, review and if necessary modify your answers (still visible on the chart) in Stage 1.

Close in prayer. If considered suitable for your group, a time of open prayer in which members can pray for the qualities, etc. listed here, will be helpful.

If not, a time of devotional silence may be helpful, during which members silently pray through what they have learned.

# OUTLINE 8

## FOR CHRIST'S SAKE
### A study on Christian suffering

## Methods to be used 8▤

Visual Aids: Dialogue.

## Equipment

Bibles (Passages to be studied – 1 Peter 3. 13–18, 1 Peter 4. 12–19).
Sheet of paper/blackboard for chart.
Felt pen/chalk.
Notepaper and pens.
Pictures of people suffering.

## Notes for Leader

1  Read Method 8 (page 28 ) for Dialogue.
2  Prepare a chart as follows: (allowing 14 lines approx.)
   *Advice to Christians when suffering*
   | *Do* | *Do not* | *Correct attitude* |

3  Become familiar with the passages, and during dialogue, ensure that the group does not wander far from the text.
4  Collect various pictures of people suffering, e.g. road accidents, starvation, hospital patients, a street fight, bomb damage.

## Presentation to the group

1  Introduction to the first letter of Peter.
   This letter is written by Peter, who was very closely associated with Jesus in His life on earth, was near Him at His trial, and who saw Him after the resurrection. He is writing to scattered groups of believers, living as a small minority in a largely non-Christian community. He instructs them in the practical aspects of living out the Christian faith, suggesting specifically how they can cope with trials and suffering, even undeserved suffering. The letter was probably written from Rome in the reign of Nero, before the outburst of persecution there in A.D. 64.
2  Opening prayer.

3  Using a picture of people suffering (e.g. from starvation, bomb or earthquake damage), point out the difference between suffering of this kind and that which provoked Peter's letter. Do not allow the group to sidetrack into discussing the philosophical problems of suffering — leave that for another study!

4  Read the two passages.

5  Fasten up the prepared chart, explaining that Peter gives advice to Christians who suffer for the sake of their faith. Work through the passages, finding the advice and filling in the chart, which will then look something like this.

*Advice to Christians when suffering for their faith*

| | Do | Do not | Correct attitude |
|---|---|---|---|
| Ch. 3 | 13 Be zealous | 14 Fear<br>Be troubled | |
| | 15 Reverence Christ<br>Prepare to make<br>defence | | 15 Gentle and<br>reverent |
| | 16 Keep conscience<br>clear | | |
| Ch. 4 | | 12 Be surprised | |
| | 13 Rejoice | 15 Murder, steal,<br>do wrong, make<br>mischief | |
| | 16 Glorify God | 16 Be ashamed | |
| | 19 Do right<br>Entrust soul to<br>faithful Creator | | |

6  With reference to the chart, consider the following questions:
Do you think that people sometimes think that they are suffering because of their faith when in fact they are suffering because of their wrong attitudes or actions? Can you give any examples?
Are people anywhere in the world today persecuted for their faith by death or imprisonment?
In what ways do you suffer for your faith?
What positive value does this kind of suffering have?
Which piece of advice do you think is most helpful for us?

7  Working in twos or fours, prepare dialogues between Peter and someone who said that he had suffered more since he became a Christian than before. Since he now lived a far better life, he could not understand this and was rather resentful. Peter should make use of as many points as possible from the passages under review, but the other speaker may use any points he can think of.
Allow up to ten minutes for this, and hand out notepaper and pens if needed.

8  Hear all or some of the dialogues, and discuss, if time permits.

9  Summarize and close in prayer, praying for Christians in countries where they suffer severely for their faith.

153

# OUTLINE 9

## WHERE IS LOVE?
## A study on neighbourly love

## Method 7

Interview (with acknowledgments to Scripture Union Sunday School Department).

## Equipment

Bibles (Passages to be studied – Luke 10. 25–37).
Note pad and pens.
Map of Palestine (may be printed, or home made).

## Notes for leader

1   Read Method 7 (page 26 ) for interview method.
2   For introductory material on Samaritans, see Outline 1 'Presentation to the Group, Introduction'.
3   The leader needs to prepare the questions for the interview carefully.
4   Allow adequate time at the end for discussion of application of the passage. Make general plans for practical action while members are enthusiastic, but leave specific planning until next meeting if time is short.

# Presentation to the group

1 *Introduction.* (Pin up map of Palestine and mark Jerusalem and Jericho.) The parable of the Good Samaritan is so well-known that we often tend to skim over it superficially. We are going to try to enter into the thoughts and feelings of the people in the story to see if we can come to a deeper understanding of it.

I want to read you what was said about it by Professor E. M. Blaiklock in the Scripture Union Bible Study Book on St. Luke.

'This story bears all the marks of truth. From Jerusalem, 2,600 feet above the sea, to Jericho is the Great Rift Valley. It was a place for bandit and highwayman, with boulders on the barren hillsides to hide the waiting thief, and deep desert to conceal his flight.

It was human enough for the priest and Levite to pass furtively by. The inert figure in the roadside dust might just have been a decoy. The high priest at Jerusalem might have counselled caution and non-involvement. How many good people in some sombre modern slum would care to repeat the scene of the Samaritan's act of mercy, with danger lurking in every corner of the sinister environment?'

That helps to put a different complexion on the situation, doesn't it? What is more, the Samaritans and the Jews did not get on together.

(See Outline 1. Presentation to the group, Introduction.)

2 Turn to and read Luke 10. vv. 25–29.

List all the things we can learn about the lawyer from these verses. (If no answers are forthcoming, lead the group step by step as follows:

Was he a religious man?

Did he know the scriptures?

Do you think he asked the question because he wanted to know the answer?

Did he mind being put in his place?

Was his religion from the heart, i.e. was he a sincere believer?

3 Read verses 30–37.

4 Make four groups, each with a leader. Hand out notepaper and pens. The leader of each group represents one of the characters in the story, and has to elicit from his group as many points as possible in his favour.

1. Priest. Collect excuses for his behaviour.

2. Levite. Collect excuses for his behaviour.

3. Traveller. Collect reasons why he should be helped.

4. Samaritan. Collect reasons for his going to help.

(Allow five minutes for this.)

5 Leader: interview each character in turn, attempting to show each one for what he is, by giving the traveller and the Samaritan every opportunity to appear in a good light, and by

demolishing the arguments of the priest and Levite, on humanitarian grounds.

(Allow up to ten minutes for this.)

6  Application

Religion should be practical.

In what ways can we as Christians show Christian love to our neighbours?

Who is our neighbour? (Be specific — not simply 'elderly people' but 'Mrs. Smith down the road'.)

What action can we take to be neighbourly? (Again, be specific.)

Is there any group project we can undertake?

Decide on definite action to be taken by the group, or by individuals, and appoint a director of operations to ensure that it is carried out.

7  Close in prayer, asking God's help in whatever is undertaken in His name.

# OUTLINE 10

## TILL DEATH US DO PART
## A study on Christian marriage

## Method 11🖍 10◻ 1🖐

Alternative methods are suggested for the introduction – AVA; extracts from books, etc.; case history.

Main part of the meeting – Question and Answer plus Buzz Groups.

## Equipment

Filmstrip 'Christian Standards', Strip 5 (Part 1 only) available from CPAS Publications, Falcon Court, 32 Fleet Street, E.C.4, at £1.50 or on loan from Church Army, 185 Marylebone Road, N.W.1.

Magazines.

Tape recording of State marriage agreement (see notes for leader).

Bibles (passages to be studied –
Genesis 2. 15–25
Eph. 5. 20–33
1 Cor. 13. 4–7)

## Notes for Leader

1 Several introductions are offered and care should be taken in selecting one which is suitable for the group. The filmstrip offers a good general introduction to the subject for any group. If all members accept the Biblical view of marriage, it will be possible to start with the Bible study, if time is limited. Where several members are likely to be unconvinced by the Biblical view, introduction (c) may prove useful. Methods (b) and (d) will be found suitable for a mixed group in which some members are inclined to the Biblical view and others are not.

2 Acquire a copy of the State marriage agreement from a Registry Office and enlist the aid of friends to make a realistic tape of a Registry Office marriage.

*Introduction* (alternatives)

(a) Show filmstrip mentioned above, or

(b) Read extracts from a book or magazine to illustrate the difficulties of married life. The problem pages of many women's magazines will provide ample material. Discuss the problem and hear the group's comments and suggestions for their solutions, or

(c) Play a tape of the State marriage agreement. Discuss its basic assumptions, and the privileges and responsibilities it gives to the couple, or

(d) Using the case history method, describe the following situation, or a similar one.

Anne, aged 19, met Dave while she was at University. Dave is a car mechanic whom she met at a University dance where he was playing in the band. They were attracted to each other and she spent a night at his home while his parents were away. She was later horrified to find that she was pregnant, but decided to leave University and marry Dave for the sake of the baby.

Her parents were very understanding and, because Dave and Anne had little money, offered to let them live with them in their home. Dave refused to leave his home town and his job and found a tiny, damp attic flat for them. They married in a Registry Office and moved in. Anne tried to make it cosy but became despondent because Dave was hardly ever in, spending a lot of time at the table tennis club with his old cronies. The baby was born and Dave could not stand the crying, so he went out more and more. Anne heard from a University friend that he had been seen around with another girl. She immediately decided to try to get a divorce by any means possible, and meanwhile went home to her parents, who welcomed her and the baby.

Discuss this situation with the group, and list where Dave and Anne went wrong. The following points may emerge: mutual attraction appeared to be mainly physical; selfishness on both sides; lack of common background and interests; marriage entered into lightly and only because of the baby; no attempt on either side to make the marriage work; possibly both too immature for marriage; Anne too eager to get back to Mum; no thought of God.

After a general discussion of the causes of the breakdown, try briefly to be constructive and to consider how Anne and Dave should have acted.

## Biblical study

Follow on from any of the introductions to a consideration of the Biblical view of marriage.

1   Read Genesis 2. 15–25.

Why did God create woman?

Do you think she still does and should fulfil the same function? How does it work out in practice? (Give specific examples, where possible.)

Why did God decree that a man should leave his father and mother when he married? What are the advantages of doing so? And what are the disadvantages if all live together? What advice would you give to a couple who could not afford to set up house on their own?

What are the implications of the statement that the two become one flesh? (With reference to the permanence of marriage, the possibility of sexual relationships with other people, the attitude of each to the partner, etc.)

2 Read Ephesians 5. 22–33.

What instruction is given to both husband and wife?

What instruction is given to (a) husband and (b) wife?

What reasons are given in both cases?

Do these instructions apply to Christians today? (Deal with each separately, if preferred.) Are they applied by Christians today?

Do they apply equally to non-Christians?

Paul describes the marriage relationship as similar to that between Christ and the Church. What does this imply about (a) The length of time a marriage should last? (b) The quality of the relationship? (c) The responsibility of the man? (d) The correct attitude to adultery?

(These questions may be dealt with in Buzz groups.)

3 Read 1 Cor. 13. 4–7.

Ask each member to comment on one phrase, and if possible to give an example of it in practice — the examples need not be limited to the marriage relationship, but should refer to it where possible. Members should be given a minute or two to sort out their thoughts before the comments and examples are heard by the whole group. Some groups may prefer to do this in twos, and specific phrases should be allocated to each person or pair.

Hear comments and discuss. Several points will emerge and should be dealt with in depth as they arise. Finally point out that a marriage worked out on this basis would be more than likely to succeed.


# General discussion

The following questions may be discussed if they have not already arisen.

Why get married? (Leader: marriage ordained by God; for the good of the individuals; for the sake of the children; for the sake of society at large, etc.)

What is wrong with trial marriages?

Should everyone expect to get married?

Do the same standards of sexual morality apply to Christians and non-Christians?

How can we know whom to marry?

What advantage has the Christian in (a) deciding who to marry, (b) married life?

Close in prayer if appropriate to the group.

# OUTLINE 11

## WHAT'S WRONG WITH THE WORLD?
### A study on social evils

## Method 1🎭 6😀 11👂

Charted lists, Questions and Answers. Dramatic writing.
Or use filmstrip 'Amos, the Prophet' (Carwal). See Method 11,
page 33 ).

### Equipment

Bibles – one set of one modern translation, preferably 'Four
Prophets' by J. B. Phillips (Bles), or NEB or RSV.
(Passages to be studied in detail – see below under 'Presenta-
tion 3'.)
Large sheet of paper for compiling list.
Felt pen.
Chart with headings (see 'Presentation 3').
Summary chart, if desired (see 'Presentation 2').
Note pad and pens.
Slips of paper with references for 'Presentation 3'.

### Notes to Leader

1   Read Method 1 (page 16 ) for Question and Answer method,
    and refer to Method 11 (page 33 ) for use of visual aids.
2   In your preparation, read the whole of Amos, in a modern
    translation.
       The following summary may be useful as you read the book,
    and for reference afterwards; it may also be put in abbreviated
    form on a chart to show to the whole group (see 'Presentation
    2').
         Ch. 1 – Ch. 2.5   Amos speaks out against all the surround-
            ing countries, for their brutality, slave trade, pitilessness,
            selfishness, etc. The Israelites would welcome such
            condemnation of their enemies.
         Ch. 2. 6–16   Amos suddenly turns to Israel herself and
            declares that she is evil in her ways, too. The Lord has
            helped her in war, but will punish her for turning against
            Him.
         Ch. 3   Amos foresees the punishment.
         Ch. 4   The women, who love luxury, will suffer a terrible
            fate.
            Verses 4–5   Irony – 'go and get on with your sinning'.
            Although the Lord has tried to bring Israel to her senses,

she has ignored Him, and must now prepare to meet Him.

Ch. 5. 1–2   A lament for Israel.

Verse 3   God's warning.

Verses 4–5   God's advice.

Verses 6–15   Fear the Lord. Evil men will not prosper.

Verses 16–20   If you continue to do evil, there will be disaster.

Verse 21–24   God requires justice and integrity, not sacrifices.

Ch. 6   God will punish complacency and pride.

Ch. 7. 1–9   Visions of locusts and drought, and a plumbline with which God will test His people, and then punish them.

Verses 10–17   Amaziah, priest of Bethel, denounces Amos, and sends him home.

Amos replies with prophecies of judgment.

Ch. 8   Vision of ripe fruit, representing Israel ripe for destruction.

Israel's lack of care for those in need will bring darkness, death and despair, and the loss of God's word.

Ch. 9   There is no escape – but there is hope in the distant future.

3   Try to keep the meeting moving quickly while the list of evils is being compiled, otherwise it will become tedious.

4   The conclusion may be amplified to cover additional issues which are current problems, and may deal with the responsibility which belongs to a Christian in a particular situation.

5   Because of the length of the outline it may be helpful to devote two meetings to it.

## Presentation to the group

1   Introduction.

We tend to think that the social and moral problems of our day are new. The prophet Amos, in the 8th century B.C., spoke out against the same sort of thing. He was a shepherd from Tekoa in Judah who came to Bethel, in Israel, and saw there material prosperity accompanied by social and moral depravity, oppression of the poor, and religious insincerity. He was so incensed that he spoke out against it openly in the market place of Bethel. He collected a crowd by first denouncing the surrounding countries before turning his attention to Israel. He was eventually sent home by the priest of Bethel, because the people could not bear the accusations.

The situation in Israel in the 8th century B.C. was in some ways similar to that in Britain today – affluence and prosperity coupled with a decay in moral standards and religious belief. However, Israel was in a special relationship to God, as His chosen nation. There was still a known framework of standards to which Amos could appeal.

2 Summarize the book of Amos – either by reading a summary, showing it on a chart, or flicking through the pages together.

3 All together, read the following sections, and compile on a chart a list of the evils denounced. Hand out to individuals slips of paper with the references so that they are prepared beforehand to read aloud. As each reference is read, ask the group to call out the evils mentioned, and you write them on the chart as they occur.

Chap. 2. 6–8   Social injustice.
Idolatry and sacred prostitution.
Unjust dealings.

Ch. 4. 1, 4–5   Luxurious living, oppression of the poor.
Religious insincerity.

Ch. 5. 10–13   Dishonesty in courts
Profiting by the poor.
Taking bribes.

Ch. 5. 21–24.   Sacrifice without right attitude of heart and life.

Ch. 6. 4–6   Thoughtless luxury.

Ch. 8. 4–5   Oppression of poor.
More eager for unjust gain than for worship.
Dishonest trading.

*Do these evils still occur today?*

4 What advice is repeated three times in Ch. 5?
What practical results should this have had in Israel's national life?

5 Does God still require these things? Can we expect to see them in our society? If not, why not?

6 If Amos came to a big city in Britain today, what would he say? Divide into groups of three or four and spend ten minutes preparing notes of a speech to be made by Amos today. Remember that Amos gave positive advice as well as pointing out and denouncing sin!
(Hear one or two speeches, from members who can put it over effectively.)

7 *Conclusion*
Turn to Ch. 3. 2   Why did the Israelites have special responsibilities?
Do we as Christians have special responsibilities? (Be specific.)

Close in prayer, asking for forgiveness for national and individual sins, and for strength to carry out responsibilities as a Christian.

## Set two

## Study outlines on Paul's letter to the Colossians

## Notes to Leader

1   The following is a systematic study of the whole of the letter to the Colossians, using the Question and Answer method, and is suitable for use in a series of four or five meetings. It is divided into headed sections which can be grouped in various ways to form a series of studies, depending on the length of time and number of meetings available.

2   The leader may be the sole possessor of the outline; if a typewriter and duplicator are available, copies may be made for each member of the group. If this is done, it is recommended that every alternate page be left blank for the member to write notes. Quarto sheets used sideways and stapled together in book form are suitable.

3   The leader should read as many commentaries on the letter as are available to him. The Tyndale commentary on Colossians and Philemon and the Scripture Union Bible Study Book on Ephesians, Philippians, Colossians and Thessalonians are particularly helpful.

4   The outlines are based on Today's English Version, Good News for Modern Man, copies of which should be available to all members of the group. Other versions will be useful for comparison, but it is helpful if the study is done from one version.

5   It is recommended that each section should be read aloud by one member of the group prior to its study.

6   If members are in possession of a copy of the outline, they should be encouraged to spend some of the study time working alone or in twos, jotting down notes on the blank pages. The notes may be preparatory to the general discussion or a summary of it.

## Introduction

It is generally agreed that the letter was written by Paul to the Christians at Colossae in A.D. 62 or 63, from prison in Rome. (See commentaries for further details and theories.)

The letter is an attempt to refute several false ideas which had arisen. In the first century A.D. there was a tendency to syncretize, or mix various philosophies, and Christianity at Colossae was being affected by this. The false ideas which were being incorporated into Christianity were:

1   The widely held belief that body and spirit were in opposition, which resulted in a tendency either to subdue the body by rigorous law-keeping and abstinence, or to live licentiously

163

on the basis that the body was not important. Paul in this letter deals with the problem of rigorous and unnecessary observance of the Jewish law.

2   The misconception that Jesus is merely one of the several angelic beings who mediate between man and God. In a magnificently rich statement, Paul describes the unique person and work of Jesus.

3   Knowledge was highly thought of and was considered to be available only to the few. Paul points out that the gospel of Jesus Christ is for all, and that He is the key to all the hidden treasures of God's wisdom and knowledge.

## Ch. 1. 1–2   Introduction to epistle

Comment briefly, or elicit comments from the group, on the following words.

Abbreviated suggestions or suitable comments are given in brackets.

| | |
|---|---|
| apostle | (one sent out with authority.) |
| God's people | ('Saints' in many translations.) |
| in Christ | (Well-known Pauline phrase with many associations – someone 'in Christ' is a Christian.) |
| grace | (undeserved favour from God.) |
| peace | (state of mind resulting from being in God's favour.) |

## Ch. 1. 3–8   Thanksgiving

| | |
|---|---|
| Hope | What did the Christians in Colossae hope for? What do Christians today hope for? What do other people hope for? Is there a difference between the kinds of hope? (The hope of the Christian is a *sure* hope.) |
| Blessings | How would you describe the blessings of the gospel in the world today? (Many translations use the word 'fruit' for blessings.) |

## Ch. 1. 9–14   Paul's Prayer

What two things does Paul pray for them? (verse 9 and verse 11).

What does Paul say will be the results of the first thing he prays for them?

What does he say they should give thanks for? (verses 12–14).

How can we set about trying to be filled with the knowledge of God's will?

How far are the lives of Christians today fruitful in all kinds of good works?

What is the power of darkness, and how does it affect people today?

What is the kingdom of His Son?

## Ch. 1. 15–20   The Person and Work of Christ

What do we learn in these verses about how Christ is related to
   (a) God the Father?
   (b) the Universe?
   (c) the Church?

(Groups of two and three members may discuss these separately. A similar procedure may be adopted with the following three questions.)

'In order that He alone might have the first place in all things, (v. 18) — if we really believe this, what difference will it make to the way we think about

    (*a*)  our careers?

    (*b*)  our leisure?

    (*c*)  our relationships with other people?

*Ch. 1. 21–23  The Work of Christ Applied to the Colossians*

How can God bring sinful people as 'pure, holy and innocent' into His presence?

What practical ways are there in which we can try to continue faithful? (v. 23).

*Ch. 1. 24 – Ch. 2. 5  Paul's part in God's Plan*

Paul's task was fully to proclaim the message.

The message is that God has revealed His secret.

The secret is Christ in you.

Paul's aim was to bring each person into God's presence as a mature individual in union with Christ.

What would you suggest are the basic requirements for Christian maturity?

*Ch. 2. 6 – Ch. 3. 4  Fullness of Life in Christ*

*1. vv. 6–10*

How can we try to keep our roots deep in Him (vv. 6–7)?

We need to beware of being made captive by human wisdom. What examples of dangerous human wisdom are around us today?

    Does this mean that Christians should be ignorant of modern philosophy and thought?

Our fullness of life comes from union with Him, who is fully God and fully man — what difference does this fullness of life make in practical terms?

*2. vv. 11–15  Christ's work is complete*

Paul sums up all that God has done for them in Christ. What was their state before they became Christians, and how has the change come about?

*3. Ch. 2. 16 – Ch. 3. 4  The dangers of being sidetracked*

What are the apparent advantages of guiding your life by a set of rules?

What reason does Paul give for saying this is wrong?

What are the things which are likely to sidetrack us in a similar way today?

In what practical ways can we set our hearts on the things that are in heaven?

*Ch. 3. 5–17  The Old Life and the New*

*1. vv. 5–11*

How can we practically set about 'putting to death' the things listed in 5–9?

If we have 'put on the new self', does this mean we automatically live lives which are pleasing to God?

Why do we still need to 'put to death' the various sins?

*2. vv. 12–17*

Paul describes the kind of character the Christian should try to cultivate.

How should this show itself in everyday life?

How should it affect our attitudes to (a) other people, (b) circumstances, (c) God?

(These questions may be discussed in small groups.)

*Ch. 3. 18 – Ch. 4. 1    Personal Relationships*

Paul emphasizes that it is the Lord who should control all our relationships, but in practice we often find it difficult to know exactly what He wants us to do.

Working in small groups, think of situations where there appears to be a conflict of loyalties and try to decide what it is right to do.

(Leader: if the groups have difficulty in thinking of situations, give them written examples to discuss – e.g. parent forbids young person to attend church, teacher or works manager asks you to do something you believe is wrong.)

*Ch. 4. 2–6    Instructions*

What do these verses teach about (a) prayer, (b) conduct, (c) speech?

(Discuss in small groups, and then briefly compare answers and discuss together.)

*Ch. 4. 7–18    Christian Fellowship in Action*

How do these verses show Christian fellowship working out in practice?

How can your church/youth fellowship/school group/college group/works CU/etc. demonstrate practical Christian fellowship (a) among your own members, (b) outside the group?

Give practical suggestions as far as possible.

# SECTION 3
# Part B

## Brief outlines

In the following outlines, only a sketchy summary of the procedure is described and, after the first one, the introduction, prayer and summary are taken for granted. The aim is to give the leader some help in his preparation, but to allow him scope for adaptation of the outlines to his own group's requirements, and opportunity to use his own ideas.

## Contents

# Old Testament teaching and prophecy

1 *Deut. 8. 1–20  An affluent society*
        Basic Doctrines Method (p. 18 )
   *Introduction.* The children of Israel had been led from Egypt by Moses and kept safe by God for forty years in the wilderness. Before taking possession of the promised land, they are given God's instructions about how they are to conduct themselves.

   In some ways the situation they were promised is similar to that in Western countries today – we are affluent, but we tend as nations to forget God.

   *Read* the passage – preferably using at least two readers, who can read in a lively way.

   *Pray* for understanding.

   *What is the passage basically about?*
        (God's good gifts, need for gratitude, etc.)
   *What does it teach about God?*
        (Make list on wall chart or in note books)
   *What does it teach about life?* i.e.
        What commands are there? (Make list)
        What promises are there? (Make list)
        What warnings are there? (Make list)
   Application:
        In what ways is our situation similar?
        Are we as Christians grateful for all that God has done for us?
        Should we expect non-Christians to be grateful to God?
        What is the message for us today?
        Summarize.
        Close in prayer.

2 *Joshua 24. 1–28  Freedom of Choice*
        Key Questions (p. 19 )
        AVA (p. 33 )
   *Read* vv. 1–13 and summarize – or leaders summarize, by way of introduction or depict events on a flannelgraph.
   *Read* vv. 14–28 either in paragraphs, or with a narrator, Joshua, and people.
        What are the reasons given for serving the Lord?
        What is required of those who do serve the Lord?
        Have we today a simple choice between God and other gods. If so, what are the other gods?
        What is required of us when we decide to serve the Lord?
        Are people in general aware that they must make a choice?
        Taking our example from Joshua, what can we do to let them know? What else can we do?

3 *Isaiah 53  The Coming Messiah*
        AVA (p. 33 )
        Group Preparation (p. 44 )
        Key Questions (p. 19 )
   *Beforehand.* All read the passage, and from the gospel stories

note the fulfilments of the prophecies.

This may be done by writing out Isa. 53 on the left-hand page of a note book and noting the gospel fulfilments on the right-hand page, parallel with the relevant prophecies.

*At the meeting.* Discuss the meaning of the prophecies, using questions such as

Why was He despised and rejected (v. 3)?

How has He borne our griefs (v. 4)?

How has His chastisement made us whole (v. 5)?

Why has the Lord laid on Him the iniquity of us all (v. 6)?

Discuss the ways in which the prophecies were fulfilled, sharing findings from the preparation beforehand.

*How does it affect us today?*

N.B. The following filmstrip may be used as a conclusion and summary:

'Prophecies' (Filmbooks Ltd.). The notes quote Old Testament prophecies concerning the Messiah and the pictures illustrate their fulfilment in scenes from the New Testament. Colour. Available from Church Army — See Bibliography Method 11.

4   *Isaiah 55   Seek the Lord while He may be found*
              Swedish Method (p. 21 )

*Read* the passage. *Note* on cards the points which are not understood and those calling for action. Discuss the former as necessary, and spend the majority of the time in consideration of the meaning of the points requiring action, and how to put them into practice.

Finally, either in the meeting, or afterwards, each member should note points which have been clarified by the study of the passage.

5   *Ezekiel 34   The Bad Shepherds and the Good Shepherd*
              Key Questions (p. 19 )

(Have on display, pictures of sheep, shepherds, sheepfolds, etc.)

*Read* the passage.

Individually, in small groups, or in the full group using a wall chart, list the stated qualities of a bad shepherd and a good shepherd. Apply each point to Christian leaders and work out what they should and should not do. Give examples.

*In what ways did Christ fulfil the requirements of a Good Shepherd?*

(See also John 10 and Outline 35.)

# Old Testament life stories

6   *Genesis 12–18, 20–23; 25. 1–11   Abraham, Man of Faith*
              Interview Method (p. 26 )

Either read all chapters and compile a list of characteristics shown by Abraham. Discuss whether he was a likeable man, a good father, what his faith in God consisted of, etc.

Or take selected chapters and study in detail, e.g.
Ch. 12. 1–9   The call and the promise.
Abram took a step of faith. What could have made him hesitate, had he had less faith in God?
In what ways does God call us?
Would we be so unquestioning in answering God's call?
Ch. 22. 1–19   The testing of Abraham.
Prepare an interview with Abraham, and a separate interview with Isaac, establishing their thoughts and feelings during the course of the incident.
Discuss how your reactions would compare with theirs in a similar situation.

7   *Gideon. Judges 6. 8–28   Man of Action*
Dramatization (p. 23 )
AVA (p. 23 )
Prepare a play with the following scenes:
Prologue   6. 1–10.
Scene 1   6. 11–24   Gideon is assured of his call.
Scene 2   6. 25–32   He pulls down the altar of Baal.
Scene 3   6. 33–40   He prepares for battle.
Scene 4   7. 1–8   The army is reduced to 300.
Scene 5   7. 9–25   Victory.
Scene 6   8. 1–21   The enemy killed.
Scene 7   8. 22–28   Gideon asked to become ruler.
Discuss Gideon's attitude at the various stages; the reasons for victory; the effect Gideon had on others, etc.
The play may be put on tape and played to another group to help their study of the life of Gideon.
The following filmstrip may be shown to introduce the subject matter:
Gideon, The Liberator (Concordia Productions), available from Church Army. For address, see Bibliography to Method 11.

8   *1 Kings 3   Solomon, the Wise King*
Question and Answer (p. 16 )
List and consider the good qualities shown by Solomon in his dream and in the incident.
Do the majority of people today accept these qualities as good ones?
Do we try to live up to these standards?
Are the standards any different from the standards set up by Christ, e.g. in the Sermon on the Mount?

9   *2 Kings 5   Naaman*
Newspaper report (p. 29 )
Prepare an edition of a newspaper, including a description of Naaman's visit to Elisha, a brief account of what leprosy is, an editorial on the significance of the incident, and interviews with the maid, one of Naaman's servants, and Gehazi.

# Old Testament simple narrative

10 *Genesis 3   The Fall*
              Key Questions (p. 19 )
   List the factors which influenced the woman and made her eat the fruit.
   What was the basic reason for her disobedience?
   What were the results of her disobedience?
   What is the significance for us?

11 *Isaiah 6   The call of Isaiah*
              Question and Answer (p. 16 )
              Mime (p. 23 )
   This passage may be effectively mimed while a narrator reads it aloud. This is best done after the incident has been studied in detail.
   Questions for discussion:
     What do we learn about God?
     What effect does He have on men?
     What is required of us before God calls us?
     How does God's call come to us today?
     Do we respond as readily as Isaiah did?

# Old Testament dramatic incident

12 *Exodus 32   The Golden Calf*
              Dramatization (p. 23 )
              Question and Answer (p. 16 )
   The incident may be made into a play with scenes based on the following verses:
   1–6, 7–14, 15–20, 21–29, 30–35.
   In addition, or as an alternative, the following questions may be discussed:
   Why was the golden calf made?
   What was wrong with making it?
   What does the incident teach us about God?
   In what ways can we be said to have golden calves today?
   Is this true only of non-Christians, or are Christians equally guilty?

13 *1 Samuel 17   David and Goliath*
              Key Questions (p. 19 )
              AVA (p. 33 )
              Dramatization (p. 23 )
              Interview (p. 26 )
   The incident may be dramatized, or an interview (e.g. for the 'Philistine Gazette', or the Israel Television Service) may be prepared with one of the onlookers. This may be put on tape. Alternatively it may be taped beforehand by the leader and others and played as an introduction to the subject.

In addition, or as an alternative, the following questions may be discussed:

List on paper or on a wall chart, the advantages Goliath had and the disadvantages David had in the fight? Why did David win? What does the incident teach about the respective power of good and evil?

Does good always triumph?

What kind of person does David show himself to be, in this incident?

14 *1 Kings 18   Elijah versus the Priests of Baal*
Dramatization (p. 23 )
Dramatize, with scenes as follows:
Verses 1–6, 7–19, 20–29, 30–40, 41–46.

In addition, or as an alternative, the following questions may be discussed:

'How long will you go lingering with two different opinions?' (v. 21).

Do people do this today, with reference to
(a) Jesus?
(b) Other issues?

If so, why do they do it?

How can we help people to reach a decision about Jesus?

15 *Nehemiah 1–6   Rebuilding the Walls of Jerusalem*
Character Study (p. 39 )
Dialogue (p. 28 )
AVA (p. 33 )

Reading a chapter at a time, build up a character study of Nehemiah.

Additional questions:

In chapter 1 what are the elements of Nehemiah's prayer?

What can this teach us about prayer?

What qualities of Nehemiah made him a good leader?

Why were the Jews successful in their enterprise?

or

Prepare a conversation about the events between:
(*a*) One of the returned Jews and his wife, one evening after the wall has been finished.
(*b*) Sanballat and one of his officials when they hear the wall has been started.
(*c*) Nehemiah explaining to a friend in Susa how he overcame his difficulties.

The following filmstrip may be used to summarize the incident:

'Nehemiah' (Educational Production Ltd.) – The story of the rebuilding of Jerusalem under Nehemiah, and of the revived faith of its inhabitants. Available from Church Army. For address see Bibliography to Method 11.

# Old Testament poetry

16 *Psalm 103*
> Comments (p. 41 )

Read aloud, slowly and thoughtfully.

Spend ten to fifteen minutes considering the psalm, either individually in silence, or in pairs.

Working systematically through the psalm, let each person comment on a verse, or group of verses.

17 *Isaiah 40   Behold your God*
> Key Questions (p. 19 )

Consider and discuss all that can be learned from this chapter about God.

# Life of Christ

18 *Matt. 4. 1–11   The Temptations*
> Chart (p. 33 )

*Introduction*. The answers Jesus gives to the three temptations are quotations from Deuteronomy and they all refer to the forty years when the Israelites were tested in the wilderness before their entry into the Promised Land. The temptations of Jesus were the same in effect as those which came to the Israelites and the same which come to us all, in one way or another.
*Read* the passage.

On a previously prepared chart, write up the points made under the following headings, and discuss:

> Temptation        Meaning        Answer of Jesus

What parallels have these temptations in our own experience?
How can we overcome temptation?

19 *John 7. 14–52   Is He the Christ?*
> Dramatization (p. 23 )

Read, taking parts – narrator, Jesus, group of people, etc.
Prepare discussion held between (a) the people in vv. 25–27, (b) the people in v. 31, (c) the Pharisees, (d) believers in v. 41, (e) non-believers in vv. 41–42, (f) officers in v. 45, (g) Nicodemus.

Bring out in the discussion all the points made by the people in the passage, and any other points consistent with those expressed. Detailed study of the passage will be required, and small groups may cover different parts of the discussion, with a co-ordinator ensuring that the whole conversation holds together.
*Or*

Prepare a court hearing on the question 'Is He the Christ?' and produce, from this passage, witnesses on both sides.

Finally (for either version) *What is your verdict?*

20 *Evidence for the Resurrection, Matt. 28, Mark 16, Luke 24, John 20*

> Interview (p. 26 )
> Dramatization (p. 23 )
> Group Preparation (p 44 )
> AVA (p. 33 )

*Either*

Interview Mary Magdalene, Salome, the two on the Emmaus road, Peter, and Thomas.

Allocate each character to one group member who finds out all he can about him, and answers questions put to him by the leader acting as jnterviewer.

*Or*

Prepare a court hearing, with counsel for the prosecution and counsel for the defence, each calling witnesses. The judge should prepare a final summing-up and the jury (all group members) decide the verdict.

*Or*

All read the passages beforehand and at the meeting discuss the following questions:

What does the passage teach about:
   the fact of the resurrection
   the reason for the resurrection
   the results of the resurrection?

N.B. The meeting could be opened with a showing of the CPAS Filmstrip 'The Message of the Resurrection' (see Bibliography to Method 11 for address). Notes provided with strip. 41 frames. Contemporary style artwork. Good for all ages.

21 *Parables. Matt. 13. 3–23   The Sower*

> Visual Aid (p. 33 )

Tell the story, using a flannelgraph.

You will need a *man* (the sower), an area for the *field*, surrounded by a *path* and with areas of *rocky ground* and *thorns.* Scatter *seed* on each area. Bring on *birds* to eat up the seed from the path. Place *sun* at the top of the scene. Place *large straggly plants* on rocky ground, and then remove them.

Place healthy plants on thorny ground, but cover with large thorns. Place healthy plants on good soil and leave them there. Read verses 10–23.

Taking each of the four situations in turn, think of parallel examples from life.

What is the message of the parable for us?

22 *Matt. 21. 33–44   The Ungrateful Tenants*

> Character study (p 39 )

Divide into three groups, each finding out all it can about the householder, the tenants and the son.

Share findings.

What do we learn about God the Father, God the Son and ourselves?

Discuss how far the parallels may be drawn from this parable.

## Stories of healing

23  *Matt. 8. 5–13   A Man of Faith*
        Character Study (p. 39 )
        Question and Answer (p. 16 )
Read passage.
What sort of a man was the centurion? (Work out as many points as possible from the passages and list them on a chart.)
How did Jesus react to him?
In what ways should we be like the centurion? (Refer to the chart.)
Can we expect instant healing for ourselves or for others, if we have such faith?

24  *Mark 2. 1–12   The Paralytic*
        Newspaper (p. 29 )
Prepare an interview with the paralytic, and an account. purporting to be by one of the four men who carried him; a disapproving account by one of the scribes, and an editorial on the forgiveness of sins.
These may be prepared by the whole group or allocated to smaller groups.

25  *Mark 10. 46–52   Blind Bartimaeus*
        Dramatization (p. 23 )
Study the passage and dramatize it, with individuals taking the parts of Bartimaeus and Jesus, several as disciples and the remainder as the crowd.
Discuss what caused Jesus to heal Bartimaeus.
What can we learn from Bartimaeus?

## Other miracles

26  *John 2. 1–11   Water into Wine*
        Dramatization (p. 23 )
        Key Questions (p. 19 )
Read the passage.
Tell the story in the words of one of the servants.
What can we learn about Mary's attitude to Jesus?
Why did Jesus perform this miracle?
(Have available pictures of water jars, and any other domestic items likely to be in use at the feast.)

## Lives and incidents

27  *Nicodemus. John 3. 1–21; John 19. 38–42*

Character study (p. 39 )
Chart (p. 33 )
AVA (p. 33 )

List points learned about the character of Nicodemus.

On a previously prepared chart, list teaching about God the Father, God the Son, God the Holy Spirit, and man.

This may be done all together in the group, or four smaller groups may assemble material each on one aspect. Each group should then have a leader and a scribe. The scribe will write up the findings on the chart in front of the reassembled groups, while the leader of each group will provide any explanations, and lead discussion on the points as they are written up.

Final question: What have we learned about ourselves from this study?

N.B. As a sequel to this study, the following filmstrip may be shown: CPAS Christian Beginnings Part 1, How to become a Christian. See Bibliography Method 11 for address.

28 *Acts 3. 1–11   The Lame Man at the Gate*
Dramatization (p. 23 )

Dramatize as follows:

Scene 1   Friends place lame man at gate, explaining what they are doing and why.
Scene 2   Peter and John enter and approach the temple, talking about the events mentioned in 2. 43–47.
Scene 3   The lame man asks for a donation and Peter replies. Helps him to his feet (vv. 3–7).
Scene 4   The man enthuses about what has happened.
Scene 5   The people are amazed.

Questions for discussion:

Peter helped the lame man in a way he did not expect – Do we sometimes ask God for the wrong things?
Peter gave what he had – do we?
The man praised God first of all – do we?

29 *Stephen. Acts 6. 8–15; 7. 54 – 8. 3*
Character Study (p. 39 )
Question and Answer (p. 16 )

List on a board or chart what can be learned about Stephen from these passages.

Consulting the chart, discuss the ways in which we should be like him. Where do we fail? What can we do about it?

Are we able to 'Dispute with wisdom and with the Spirit' (6. 10)?

Would we have the same forgiving spirit in such a situation?

Are people anywhere in the world today faced with persecution for their faith? If so, what is the effect on the church in that area?

What do you think would be the result in our country if Christians were faced with death because of their faith?

30 *Mistaken for gods – Then Stoned!   Acts 14. 8–23*

Key Questions (p. 19 )

What caused the people to think Paul and Barnabas were Gods?

Why do you think Paul and Barnabas reacted so swiftly?

How did they persuade the people they were not gods?

Why did the people change their attitude so dramatically? (v. 19.)

From the whole passage, what can we learn about Paul?

Paul and Barnabas adapted the way they presented their message to meet a specific situation.

Think of situations which we can adapt the way we talk about Christianity, to make it particularly relevant at that time. How far should we be prepared to adapt to suit a particular audience?

31  *Strange Happenings at Philippi. Acts 16. 11–40*
        Dramatization (p. 23 )
        Question and Answer (p. 16 )

For younger people, this may be studied as a serial story, in five episodes:

Verses 11–15, 16–18, 19–24, 25–34, 35–40, or it may be acted, or taken as a play reading, using the same divisions.

Discussion may follow on the attitudes shown by Paul in the various situations, the effect he had on the people he met, etc.

32  *Paul's Defence before Agrippa. Acts 26. 1–32*
        Interview (p. 26 )

Re-write the chapter as an interview between Paul and a TV interviewer, in which Paul makes all the points in the passage, but only in answer to carefully-worded questions. (The aim is to make the group delve into the text.)

Small sub-groups may take a paragraph each, from which they select their questions, and the leader, or someone else who has become very familiar with the passage, takes the part of Paul. One section may be dealt with at a time, before the whole group, using a different interviewer and a different Paul for each section, or the whole interview may be held as an entity.

After the interview, there may be general discussion on the implications of the incident.

It may be helpful to have on display a map of Paul's journeys.

33  *The Holy Spirit in the Early Church and in the Church Today*
        Group Preparation (p. 44 )

Passages for study in advance: Acts 2, Acts 8. 4–24, Acts 9. 1–19, Acts 10. 1–48, Acts 19, 1–7, 1 Cor. chapters 12–14.

Discuss the following questions:

What was necessary before people could receive the Holy Spirit?

How did people know that they had received Him?

What was the purpose of the giving of the Holy Spirit?

Is there a distinction between being filled by the Spirit and receiving the Spirit?

Is there a difference between the fruit of the Spirit (Galatians 5. 22, 23) and the gifts of the Spirit (1 Cor. 12. 4–11)?

Is the Spirit at work in the same ways in the Church today? If not, why not? Should He be?

What should we do about it?

34 *The Beatitudes. Matt. 5. 1–14*

Question and Answer (p. 16 )

First, discuss the meaning of the word 'blessed'.

Then divide the group into pairs, allocating one beatitude to each pair, asking them to consider its meaning and to work out practical examples of its application.

After a suitable length of time, hear and discuss each pair's findings.

Finally, in full group discuss the meaning and implications of 'You are the salt of the earth' and 'You are the light of the world'.

35 *The Door and The Good Shepherd. John 10. 1–18*

Question and Answer (p. 16 )

(See Section 3, 5 on Ezekiel 34.)

What are the characteristics of a good shepherd mentioned here?

How does Jesus fulfil those requirements?

Why does Jesus refer to Himself as 'the door'? In what ways is He a door?

Where does the door lead from and to? Who may use it? (Discuss in small groups.)

Why did Jesus 'lay down His life'?

What can we learn (about our own relationship with Jesus) from this passage?

36 *Peace with God. Romans 5. 1–19*

Tape (p. 33 )

Charts (p. 33 )

Hire from Keswick Tape Library (see Bibliography to Method 11) the tape of John Stott expounding Romans 5.

Prepare four charts beforehand and fill in during the meeting, the details given here in brackets.

### Chart 1

| vv. 1–2 | Results of Justification | When received |
|---|---|---|
| | (Peace) | (Past – when converted) |
| | (Grace) | (Present – continuing) |
| | (Glory) | (Future) |

vv. 3–4 Stages  (suffering) (endurance) (character) (hope)
in Just-
ification

v. 5  How can we be sure of the future glory?

### Chart 2

vv. 6–8  Christ died for us – (List our characteristics)

Chart 3

vv. 9–11     *Present Justification*     *Final Salvation*
  How achieved      (By His death  By His life)
  People who receive (God's enemies  Now God's friends –
                               that is, those who have
                               been reconciled to Him)

Chart 4

vv. 12–19   *Adam's deed*            *Christ's deed*
  Its motive
  v. 15a      (Self-assertion       Self-sacrifice)
  Its effect
  vv.15b–17 (Death and condemnation Life and Righteousness)
  Its nature   (Disobedience        Obedience)

37 *1 Cor. 15 The Resurrection*
              Charts (p. 33 )
              Dialogue (p. 28 )
  (a) vv. 1–11   What does Paul teach about Jesus? (in pairs, list on paper). Briefly compare answers and discuss their meaning.
  (b) vv. 12–19   In pairs, prepare a conversation, with one member holding the view that there is no resurrection from the dead, the other using Paul's arguments from the passage. Rehearse and hear all versions.
  (c) vv. 51–58   What is the victory? Can we claim it for ourselves? If so, how?

38 *New Life. Ephesians 2. 1–10*
              Chart (p. 33 )
  List on a chart our state before and after conversion.
  What has God done for us?
  (See also full Outline No. 5.)

39 *Christian Humility. Philippians 2. 1–18*
              Basic Doctrines (p. 18 )
  What is the passage basically about?
  What does it teach about God – Father, Son and Holy Spirit?
  What does it teach about life – is there a command, promise, warning? – an example to follow, or an error to avoid?
  (See also full Outline No. 7.)

40 *Christian Leaders. Titus 1. 5–16*
              Case History (p. 31 )
  Section (A)
  What are the characteristics of a person accepted by the world at large as a good leader? (Work in pairs and make list.)
  Compare answers and make a composite list of the main points.
  Section (B)
  Read passage.

List characteristics of a Christian leader as mentioned here.

Section (C)

Compare lists and discuss the significance of the similarities and differences.

Conclusion

What is the message here for us?

41 *The Runaway. Philemon*
    Case History (p. 31  )

Section (A)

Tell the following story in your own words:

A twelve year old boy runs away from boarding school. Mr. Christian finds him and sends him back to the school, where the headmaster has recently become a Christian.

Compose a letter from Mr. Christian to the headmaster which the boy will take back with him.

Section (B)

Read Philemon and compare what Paul said in that situation with what you have said in your letter.

Section (C)

Discuss Paul's approach and consider what we can learn from it.

42 *Snobbery. James 2. 1–13*
    Case History (p. 31  )

Section (A)

You are the minister of a church with a regular but small membership. One Sunday, two strangers arrive at the service. One is a tramp, obviously under-nourished and dirty. The other is a well-to-do gentleman who rolls up in a Jaguar. The majority of the church members welcome the well-to-do-man with enthusiasm, but ignore the tramp.

In your next sermon you feel you must point out the error of their ways. Working in small groups, work out what kind of things you would say.

Section (B)

Read passage. What points does James emphasize in a similar situation?

Conclusion

What can we learn from this?

## Additional brief outlines (nos. 43–47)

using case history method (p. 31  )

43 *Acts 5. 1–11. Honesty Before God*
    Case History

Alan Smith was doing very well in business and as a man of some standing in the church he felt it his duty to make a gift to the church of several hundred pounds. This he did, but on his income tax declaration form he declared it as a business expense in order to get tax rebate.

He said that the church had the money and he might as well

180

make a bit on the side for himself. He felt that it wasn't wrong, because he had given such a lot of money away quite voluntarily.

Consideration of Case History

Was Alan Smith doing anything wrong?

Bible Study

Read Acts 5. 1–11. What principles emerge?

Reconsideration

Look again at the case history in the light of the principles. Think of other situations in which the same principles would apply?

## 44 *Gifts and Graces. Romans 12. 3–8 and 1 Cor. 12. 12–31a*

Case History

Mrs. Jefferson is the very capable chairman of the Women's Meeting at her church and has held this office for seven years. She has a great sense of her own importance and tends to lord it over other members – especially over those whom she feels are less capable.

Mrs. Illingworth is the secretary and although she is efficient she feels inadequate and repeatedly offers to resign to make way for someone else. She is constantly apologizing quite unnecessarily.

Mrs. Mather is social secretary and makes arrangements for all outside activities – excursions, visits to the theatre, etc. She feels that her job is the most important because the activities which she organizes are better supported than the regular meetings. Some members resent her feeling of importance because they see the social activities as less valuable than what they call the 'spiritual' meetings.

Mrs. Atkinson is the treasurer and constantly gets the books into a muddle. She resents any interference and says that no one else could do the job better.

Mrs. Sims makes the tea, arriving early each week to prepare it and staying on to wash up. She is content to do this and likes to feel useful. She does not always go into the meetings because she does not understand much of what is said and, as she has difficulty in reading, she cannot sing the hymns. Some members tend to look down on her because of this and do not treat her like one of themselves.

Mrs. Read is not on the committee, having resigned some years ago when her husband was ill. She is a very regular attender and can be relied upon to take the chair if Mrs. Jefferson does not arrive in time, or to meet a visiting speaker, or help to serve the tea if Mrs. Sims becomes flustered.

Consideration of Case History

Discuss the attitudes of each of these ladies in turn and consider what advice could be given to each.

Bible Study

Read Romans 12. 3–8 and 1 Cor. 12. 12–31a.

What principles emerge? (Have a right assessment of your own importance; use the gifts you have been given; all members have a unique function; all are necessary; interdependence; one suffers, all suffer.)

Reconsideration

In the light of these two passages, what modifications would you make in the advice you have given to the ladies?

Can you think of situations close to you where this advice would be useful?

### 45 *To Eat or Not To Eat. Romans 14*

Case History

Dianne and Lynda move from another district and join the local Young People's Fellowship. Both are vegetarians and are eager to convince other people that it is wrong to eat meat because there is a lot of cruelty involved in rearing and killing animals for market. They frequently tell the others that it is wrong and un-Christian to eat meat because members of God's creation are being caused to suffer. Pete welcomes the girls enthusiastically because he sees opportunties for lively arguments.

Sandy and Jim despise the girls and call them weak and soft. Olwyn and Stephen goad the girls by bringing meat sandwiches instead of biscuits when it is their turn to provide evening refreshments.

Helen and Suzanne are inclined to be persuaded by the girls and do not eat meat on a Saturday picnic the YPF have. However, they do eat it at other times.

The issue becomes the main point of discussion in the YPF and there are constant arguments about it, until several members leave the group because they are sickened by it all.

Finally the curate steps in and gives a very direct Bible exposition from Romans 14.

Bible Study

Read Romans 14. What points would the curate make from this passage which are relevant to the YPF? He may be specific and refer directly to the attitude of individual members, as well as giving general principles for all. (There are at least eight relevant points in the passage.)

Reconsideration

To what other situations could these principles apply?

### 46 *Working for a Living. 2 Thess. 3. 6–15*

Case History

Several young couples rent a large house in an inner-city area in order to devote their spare time to working amongst the local gangs. For several months all goes well; each goes out to work during the day and shares in all housework and running expenses. In the evenings and at week-ends they go to the local coffee bars and try to befriend the young people there and to talk to them about Jesus Christ. After a year Stuart loses his job at the factory and for a while looks round for another. It is difficult to find one and finally he stops trying. His contributions to the running costs cease and he idles away more and more time each day until he seems incapable of working or even helping with household jobs.

How should the others react?

What should Stuart do?

Bible Study

Read 2 Thess. 3. 6–15. What teaching is given? Work for your living and do not expect to be kept; avoid an idle sponger; try to make him feel ashamed of his behaviour; warn him that he is doing wrong; do not treat him as an enemy.) N.B. It is assumed that the letter is addressed to a group of Christians in which the idle member is also a Christian.

Reconsideration

In the light of the passage modify your previous comments where necessary.

47 *Genuine Faith. James 2. 14–26*

Case history

Mr. Heatherington is the owner of a shoe factory and is a regular church attender. From time to time he arranges for an evengelist to industry to visit the factory and hold meetings for the employees who are strongly encouraged to stay on after work to talk to him. He misses no opportunity to encourage people to go to church and frequently mentions his own varied church activities, from the Bible Fellowship and Prayer Meeting to the tennis club. All his employees know of his Christian profession. His rates of pay are lower than in comparable factories but he has no difficulty finding employees because of the local unemployment problem. Any employees who give cause for complaint are treated harshly. He does not allow them to have time off on compassionate grounds and, if anyone takes a day off – even for illness – before or after their official day off, he docks two days' pay.

Discuss the situation and indicate what is wrong.

Bible Study

Read James 2. 14–26. What principles emerge from this passage?

Reconsideration

Was Mr. Heatherington's faith genuine?

What would you say if you had the opportunity to talk to him?

# APPENDICES
## Note on use of Appendices

Appendix 1 groups the different types of Biblical passage and shows which methods are suitable for use with each type.

Appendix 2 takes each of the types of Biblical passage listed in Appendix 1 and gives several examples of each.

Appendix 3 lists the usual types of Bible Study Group and shows which methods can be used by each.

Thus the prospective leader will readily be able to provide himself with material and method for any given meeting. He may first select a likely passage from Appendix 2; he will then consult Appendix 1 for methods suitable for use with that type of passage; he will consult Appendix 3 to ascertain which of those methods are suitable for use with his type of group.

In the light of his findings and his knowledge of his group, he will finally decide which method – or methods – to adopt.

Alternatively, he may adopt the reverse procedure, and select first the methods suitable for his group, then the type of passage, and finally a passage suitable for use with that method.

The appendixes will also give suggestions for possible methods to leaders who have already selected, or have had selected for them, the passages for study.

Twelve outlines are worked out in detail in Section 3, Part A, where there is in addition a set of complete outlines on Colossians.

Of the passages suggested in Appendix 2, 47 are worked out in brief outline in Section 3 of this book, Part B.

## appendix 1

**TYPES OF BIBLICAL PASSAGE**
(for details see Appendix 2)

**METHODS** (for details see sec1)

| TYPES OF BIBLICAL PASSAGE | 1 Q&A | 2 Basic Doctrines | 3 Key Q | 4 3 Q | 5 Swedish | 6 Drama | 7 Interview | 8 Dialogue | 9 News paper | 10 Case History | 11 A.V.A | 12 Character Study | 13 Comments | 14 20 Q | 15 Team games | 16 Prep. before |
|---|---|---|---|---|---|---|---|---|---|---|---|---|---|---|---|---|
| O.T. Teaching & Prophecy | xxx | xxx | xxx | xxx | xxx | o | x | xx | o | x | xxx | o | xxx | xx | x | xxx |
| Lives | xxx | xx | xxx | xxx | xxx | xxx | xxx | o | xxx | xxx | xxx | xxx | xxx | xx | xx | xxx |
| Simple narrative | xx | xx | xxx | xx | o | x | xx | o | x | x | xxx | xx | xxx | xxx | x | xxx |
| Dramatic incident | xxx | xx | xxx | xxx | o | xxx | xxx | x | o | xxx | xxx | xxx | xxx | xx | x | xxx |
| Poetry | xxx | xx | xxx | xx | o | x | o | x | xxx | xxx | xxx | xxx | xxx | xxx | o | xxx |
| N.T. Life of Christ | xxx | xxx | xxx | xxx | xx | xxx | xxx | o | xx | xxx | xxx | xxx | xxx | xx | xx | xxx |
| Parables | xxx | xxx | xxx | xxx | xxx | xx | xxx | o | xxx | x | xxx | xxx | xxx | xxx | o | xxx |
| Healing stories | xxx | x | xxx | xxx | x | xxx | xxx | o | xx | x | xxx | xx | xxx | xx | o | xxx |
| Other miracles | xxx | x | xxx | xxx | x | xxx | xxx | o | xxx | x | xxx | xxx | xxx | xx | x | xxx |
| Lives & incidents | xxx | xxx | xxx | xx | x | xxx | xxx | o | xxx | xxx | xxx | xxx | xxx | xxx | x | xxx |
| Teaching | xxx | xxx | xxx | xxx | xxx | o | o | xx | o | x | xxx | o | xxx | xxx | xx | xxx |

**KEY**  xxx Very suitable  xx Suitable  x May be used, but not generally recommended  o unsuitable

# APPENDIX 2
## Examples of types of Biblical passage
(listed on chart on page 185)

### Old Testament teaching and prophecy

Deuteronomy (selections) especially
| | |
|---|---|
| 8. 1–20 | Remember the Lord your God who brought you to a good land. |
| 26. 1–11 | The first fruits. |
| 30. 11–20 | The choice between life and death. |

Joshua
| | |
|---|---|
| 24. 1–28 | Choose this day whom you will serve. |

Ecclesiastes
| | |
|---|---|
| 2. 1–11 | Pleasure and possessions. |

Isaiah
| | |
|---|---|
| 1 | God's response to a sinful people. |
| 5 | The parable of the vineyard. |
| 9. 1–7 | |
| 11. 1–10 | The coming of the Messiah prophesied. |
| 53 | |
| 43 | The Lord is Redeemer. |
| 55 | Seek the Lord while He may be found. |

Jeremiah
| | |
|---|---|
| 7. 1–28 | Amend your ways. |
| 18. 1–11 | The potter and the clay. |
| 31. 31–34 | The New Covenant. |

Ezekiel
| | |
|---|---|
| 34 | Bad leaders likened to bad shepherds. |
| 36. 22–32 | A new heart and a new spirit. |
| 37 | The valley of dry bones. |

Daniel
| | |
|---|---|
| 9. 3–19 | Daniel's prayer. |

Amos
| | |
|---|---|
| 2. 6–8 | |
| 4. 1, 4–5 | |
| 5. 10–13, 21–24 | Social evils. |
| 6. 4–6 | |
| 8. 4–5 | |

Malachi
| | |
|---|---|
| 3. 1–12 | The Lord's messenger. |

### Old Testament lives

Noah   Genesis ch. 6–9.
Abraham   Genesis ch. 12–18; 20–23; 25. 1–11.
Isaac   Genesis ch. 24; 26; 27; 35. 27–29.
Jacob (Israel)   Genesis ch. 27–35; 46. 1–7; 47. 7–12; 27–31; 48; 49.

Joseph   Genesis ch. 37 ; 39–50.
Moses, Exodus and Numbers   (selections).
Joshua   Numbers 27. 12–23 ; Joshua (selections).
Rahab and the spies   Joshua 2 ; 6. 22–25.
Achan's sin   Joshua 7 – 8. 2
Gideon   Judges 6 – 8. 28.
Samson   Judges 13–16.
Ruth   Book of Ruth.
The child Samuel   1 Samuel 1. 1–28 ; 2. 18–20, 26 ; 3. 1 – 4. 1.
David   1 and 2 Samuel (see also Dramatic Incidents).
David   1 Kings 2. 1–11.
Solomon   1 Kings 1–11 (esp. ch. 3).
Elijah   1 Kings 17–19 ; 2 Kings 1 ; 2. 1–14.
Naaman   2 Kings 5.
Daniel·  Daniel 1–6.


# Old Testament simple narrative
(see also lives)

Genesis ch. 1, 2, 3, 4.
Israel asks for a king and Saul is anointed   1 Samuel ch. 8–10.

The anointing of David   1 Samuel 16.
David and Jonathan   1 Samuel ch. 18–20.
God's promise to David   2 Samuel 7.

The building of the house of the Lord   1 Kings ch. 5–7.
The reforms of Josiah   2 Chronicles 34 ; 35. 1–6.
The call of Isaiah   Isaiah 6.
The call of Jeremiah   Jeremiah 1. 4–10.


# Old Testament dramatic incident
(see also lives)

The plagues and the escape (see sample 6)   Exodus ch. 3–14.
The golden calf   Exodus 31. 18 ; 32. 35.
Spies sent to Canaan   Numbers 13. 1–33.
Fall of Jericho   Joshua 6. 1–21.
Defeat of Kings of Moab and Canaan   Judges 3. 15–30 ; 4. 4–24.
David and Goliath   1 Samuel 17.
David and Bathsheba   2 Samuel 11. 1 – 12. 25, also Psalm 51.
Solomon's judgment   1 Kings 3. 16–28.
Visit of the Queen of Sheba   1 Kings 10. 1–13.
Widow of Zarephath   1 Kings 17. 8–24.
Elijah versus the priests of Baal   1 Kings 17. 1–7 ; 18.
Naboth's vineyard   1 Kings 21.
Return from exile and rebuilding of temple   Ezra ch. 1–6.

## Old Testament poetry

Song of Moses after escape from Egypt   Exodus 15. 1–19.
Song of Moses before his death   Deuteronomy 32, 1–43.
Song of Deborah   Judges 5. 1–31.
Hannah's prayer   1 Samuel 2. 1–10.
David's song of deliverance   2 Samuel 22. 1–51.
   Psalms 1, 5, 8, 9, 14, 18, 19, 23, 24, 25, 27, 29, 31, 32, 33, 34,
   36, 37, 40, 42, 46, 51, 62, 94, 95, 96, 97, 103, 104, 111, 119.
   1–48, 127, 136, 139.
A song of trust in the Lord   Isaiah 26.
Behold your God   Isaiah 40.

## New Testament
## Events in the Life of Christ

(see also parallel passages in other gospels.)
Birth   Matthew 1. 18 – 2. 23.
Visit to Jerusalem   Luke 2. 41–52.
Baptism   Matthew 3. 13–17.
Temptation   Matthew 4. 1–11.
Enmity of Pharisees   Matthew 12. 1–45.
Transfiguration   Matthew 17. 1–13.
Is He the Christ?   John 7. 14–52.
Entry into Jerusalem   Matthew 21. 1–17.
Anointing at Bethany   Matthew 26. 6–13.
Last Supper   Matthew 26. 17–29; John 13. 1–38.
Garden of Gethsemane   Matthew 26. 36–56.
Trial   Matthew 26. 57–68; 27. 1–31.
Crucifixion   Matthew 27. 32–66.
Resurrection   Matthew 28. 1–20.
Ascension   Acts 1. 1–11.

## New Testament parables

Parables of the kingdom   Matthew 13. 1–23;  13. 24–52;
   18. 23–35; 20. 1–16; 21. 28–44; 22. 1–14; 25. 1–30.
Lost sheep   Luke 15. 1–7.
Lost coin   Luke 15. 8–10.
Prodigal son   Luke 15. 11–32.
Rich man and Lazarus   Luke 16. 19–31.
Prayer   Luke 18. 1–14; 11. 5–13.

## New Testament healing stories

Centurion's servant   Matthew 8. 5–13.
Peter's mother-in-law   Matthew 8. 14–17.
Gadarene demoniacs   Matthew 8. 28–34.
Paralytic   Mark 2. 1–12.
Jairus' daughter   Mark 5. 22–24, 35–43.
Woman with issue of blood   Mark 5, 25–34.
Epileptic   Matthew 17. 14–21.

Blind man    John 9. 1–41.
Bartimaeus    Mark 10. 46–52.

## New Testament other miracles

Water into wine    John 2. 1–11.
Stilling the storm    Matthew 8. 23–27.
Feeding five thousand    Matthew 14. 13–21.
Feeding four thousand    Matthew 15. 32–39.
Raising of Lazarus    John 11. 1–44.

## New Testament lives and incidents

John the Baptist    Luke 1. 5–25, 57–80. Matthew 3. 1–17;
    11. 2–19. Mark 6. 14–29.
Peter    Luke 5. 1–11. Matthew 14. 22–33; 16. 13–23; 26. 30–35,
    47–56; 26. 57–58, 69–75. John 21. 1–19. Acts 2. 1–42;
    4. 1–23.
Zacchaeus    Luke 19. 1–10.
Nicodemus    John 3. 1–21; 19. 38–42.
Woman of Samaria    John 4. 4–42.
Pentecost    Acts 2. 1–13 (14–36), 37–47.
Lame man at gate    Acts 3. 1–11.
Peter and John arrested and released    Acts 5. 12–42.
Stephen taken and stoned    Acts 6. 8–15; 7. 54 – 8. 3.
Saul converted    Acts 8. 1–3; 9. 1–30.
Simon the magician    Acts 8. 4–24.
Ethiopian eunuch    Acts 8. 25–39.
Peter and Cornelius    Acts 10. 1–48.
Peter imprisoned again    Acts 12. 1–19.
Mistaken for gods    Acts 14. 8–20.
The question of circumcision    Acts 15. 1–35.
Strange happenings at Philippi    Acts 16. 11–40.
Riot at Ephesus    Acts 19. 23–41.
Paul arrested at Jerusalem    Acts 21. 27 – 23. 35.
Paul's defence before Agrippa    Acts 26.
Shipwreck    Acts 27.
To Rome    Acts 28.

## New Testament
## Teaching – doctrinal and practical

Sermon on Mount    Matthew ch. 5–7.
Discipleship    Matthew 10. 5–42.
Take up your cross    Matthew 16. 24–28.
The judgment    Matthew 25. 31–46.
Signs of the end    Mark 13.
The Word    John 1. 1–18.
The Father and the Son    John 5. 19–47.
Bread of life    John 6. 25–59.
Light    John 8. 12–20; 9. 1–7.

True freedom    John 8. 31–59.
The door and the shepherd    John 10. 1–18.
The promise of the Counsellor    John 14. 15–31.
The true vine    John 15. 1–11.
Persecution    John 15. 12–27.
Impending departure    John 16. 4b–33.
Jesus prays    John 17. 1–26.
Pentecost sermon    Acts 2. 14–36.
At Solomon's porch    Acts 5. 12–32.
Stephen's defence    Acts 7. 2–53.
Paul at Antioch    Acts 14. 13–52.
Paul at Athens    Acts 17. 16–34.
All epistles.

# appendix 3

| GROUPS | 1 Q&A | 2 Basic Doctrine | 3 Key Q | 4 3 Q | 5 Swedish | 6 Drama | 7 Interview | 8 Dialogue | 9 News paper | 10 Case history | 11 A.V.A | 12 Character study | 13 Comments | 14 20 Q | 15 Team games | 16 Prep. before |
|---|---|---|---|---|---|---|---|---|---|---|---|---|---|---|---|---|
| Under 11 years + L | XX | X | XXX | O | X | X | X | O | XXX | O | XXX | XX | O | XXX | XXX | O |
| 11 – 14 years + L | XXX | XX | XXX | O | O | X | XX | XXX | XXX | X | XXX | XXX | O | XX | XXX | X |
| 14 – 16 years + BB +L | XXX | XXX | XXX | XXX | XXX | XXX | XXX | XXX | XXX | XXX | XXX | XXX | O | XXX | XX | XX |
| 14 – 16 years no BB +L | XXX | XX | XXX | X | O | XXX | XXX | XXX | XX | XX | XXX | XXX | O | X | X | X |
| 16 – 18 years + BB +L | XXX | XXX | XXX | XXX | XXX | XXX | XXX | XXX | XX | XXX | XXX | XXX | X | XX | X | X |
| 16 – 18 years + BB no L | XXX | XX | XXX | X | X | XXX | XXX | XXX | XXX | XX | XXX | XXX | O | O | O | X |
| 16 – 18 years no BB +L | XXX | XXX | XXX | XXX | XXX | XXX | XXX | XXX | XXX | XXX | XXX | XXX | X | O | O | X |
| 16 – 18 years no BB no L | XXX | XX | XXX | X | X | X | XX | X | X | XX | XXX | XXX | X | O | O | X |
| ADULTS well established gp. of Bible readers | XXX | XXX | XXX | XXX | XXX | XX | XX | XX | X | XX | XXX | XXX | XXX | XXX | XXX | XXX |
| Little or no BB + L (eg. Young wives, Evangelistic house gp. etc.) | XXX | XX | XXX | XX | X | X | XX | XX | XX | XXX | XXX | XXX | X | X | O | O |

**METHODS** (for details see sec. I)

**KEY**

| | |
|---|---|
| +L | With experienced leader |
| noL | No experienced leader |
| +BB | With Bible background |
| noBB | Without Bible background |

| | |
|---|---|
| XXX | Very suitable |
| XX | Suitable |
| X | May be used but not generally recommended. |
| O | Unsuitable. |

# BIBLIOGRAPHY

## Bible commentaries

One Volume commentaries
   Matthew Henry, New Bible Commentary, Peake, Jameson, Fawcett and Brown.
Separate volume commentaries
   Tyndale, Scripture Union Bible Study Books.
*Bible Atlas* – Nelson.

## Organizations which produce Bible Study Outlines include:

Scripture Union, 5 Wigmore Street, London W1H 0AD and ISCF (see lists below).
Inter-Varsity Fellowship, 39 Bedford Square, London, W.C.1.

## Bible Study Outlines published by Scripture Union

*The Man Who Was God* (14 outlines on the life of Christ, price 15p).
*Bible Study Outlines on various Books of the Bible* (list available, price 2½p each).
*King of Kings* (a series of visualized Bible Study outlines, each booklet containing leader's notes and 8 leaflets for group use. This material was prepared primarily for the 13–15 age-group. Each booklet costs 12½p).
Individual titles are as follows:
   *No Tinsel at Bethlehem*
   *Which Death was Different?*
   *Man dies for three days*
   *If Christ came back tomorrow*
*Human Like Us* (43 outlines on Bible characters, by Terence Kelshaw, price 40p).

## Bible Study Outlines published by the Inter-School Christian Fellowship

(the Schools Department of Scripture Union)

*The Story of Peter* (8 outlines prepared primarily for the 11–14 age-group, price 5p).
*Parables* (9 outlines prepared primarily for the 11–14 age-group, price 5p).
*We Want to Live* (3 outlines on Romans 12, 13 and 14, prepared primarily for 16–18 year-olds, price 5p, and separate outlines for the 14–16 age-group, price 8p).
*Action Bible Study* (4 outlines on Mark's Gospel, primarily for the 12–15 age-group, price 10p).
*The Hidden Force* (series of Study Outlines on the Holy Spirit, prepared originally for 16–18 year-olds, price 8p).
*Topical Bible Studies* (a series of 5 outlines for 13–15 age-group, price 7½p).
The above prices are subject to review.